The Crab Lover's Book

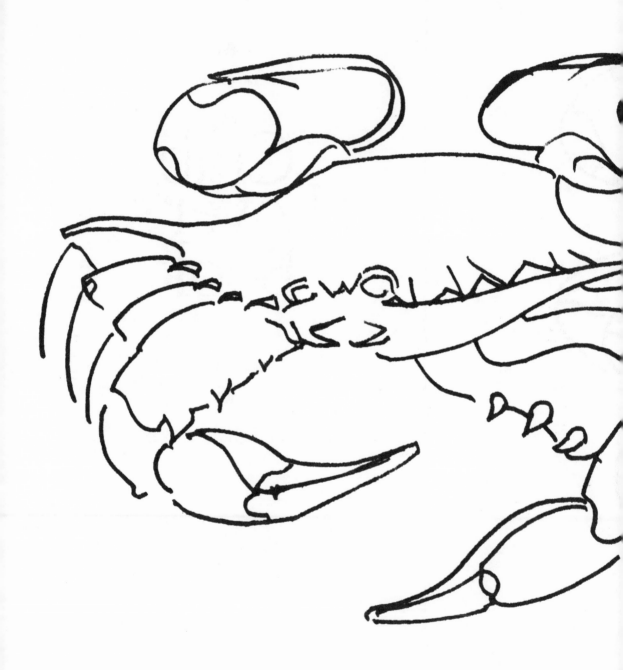

The
Crab, Lover's Book

Recipes & More

Mary Ethelyn Orso

Drawing of crab by
Walter Anderson

University Press of Mississippi / Jackson

lovingly dedicated
to my grandmother,
Marietta "Ethel" Fayard,
an extraordinary Creole cook
from Bay St. Louis, Mississippi

The figures on pages 60 and 61
are from Samuel Kirkland
Lothrop, Coclé: An
Archaeological Study of
Central Panama, *Part II*
(1942). Memoirs of the Peabody
Museum of Archaeology and
Ethnology, vol. 8. Reprinted
courtesy of the Peabody
Museum of Archaeology and
Ethnology, Harvard University.

Library of Congress Cataloging-in-
Publication Data

Orso, Mary Ethelyn.
    The crab lover's book : recipes &
    more / by Mary Ethelyn Orso.
        p.   cm.
    Includes bibliographical references
    and index.
    ISBN 0-87805-801-X.—
    ISBN 0-87805-796-X (pbk.)
    1. Cookery (Crabs)
    2. Crabs—Folklore.   I. Title.
TX754.C83077   1995
641.6'95—dc20   94-44277
                                    CIP

British Library Cataloging-in-
Publication data available

Contents

"A crabbe broke hym asonder into a dysshe make ye shells clene and put in the stuff agayne with vynegre and pouder [salt and spices] then cover it with bread [crumbs] and send it to the kytchen to hete [bake it] and broke the grete clawes and ley them in a disshe."

from an Old English cookbook by Boorde

No matter how hard the crab works to get to the top of the bushel hamper, the other crabs always pull him back down.

African-American proverb from New Orleans

Preface

This book consists of two distinctly different, but interwoven, parts. The first—the collection of recipes—grew out of a New Orleanian's love of good food. The second—the "more" part—comes from a scholar's fascination with the science and lore surrounding crabs.

The collection of recipes developed in response to requests for crab recipes from friends and family in Oregon. They were tired, they said, of "eating plain old steamed Dungeness crabs." I replied that there surely must be a cookbook of crab recipes back home in New Orleans; but if not, I promised, I would send them some so they could enjoy their Dungees in new and spicy ways.

Once back in the Big Easy, I searched in vain for a crab cookbook and so I began collecting crab recipes on my own. I wanted an eclectic assortment from several different regions and various ethnic groups.

A folklorist by profession, I collected recipes from as wide a variety of informants as possible. I gathered from family, friends, students, colleagues, neighbors, and everyone else willing to share their favorites. Gulf Coast Creole recipes passed down from my grandmother, Marietta "Ethel" Fayard, to her children and grandchildren were plentiful, and the collection, like a branching tree, began to grow and grow. If my friends in Oregon want these, it soon occured to me, others may also. I thought of my friend Joyce Mouzakis's cookbook, *The Flavor of Florence*, written to commemorate the centennial of her little Oregon seaport town, and soon I was on my way to creating *The Crab Lover's Book: Recipes & More*.

The result is a large hodge-podge of recipes in several different cooking styles. The number of servings that they produce has been approximated in portions of one cup. Since serving sizes will vary according to the cook and the situation, the crab lover cook who can afford it may wish to experiment with a recipe before serving it to the boss or the church pastor.

There are thousands of crab species, but in the United States, four types form the heart of our crab cuisine: the blue crab, the Dungeness crab, the Alaskan king crab, and the Florida stone crab. You will learn a lot about these guys in the pages that follow.

As a Louisiana native, I admit to a special fondness for blue crabs, and the book is somewhat slanted in that crustacean's direction. Louisiana seafood promoters say the state is the number one producer in the nation not only of blue crab but of many other valuable seafood species, such as shrimp, crawfish, oysters, fresh tuna, red snapper, wild catfish, black drum, seatrout, and mullet.

But it is not just the tremendous bounty of blue crabs and their relatively low cost that has resulted in an enormous cornucopia of Louisiana crab recipes; it is, rather, our state's Creole French background.

I grew up in a family of Creole French ancestry that placed a tremendous emphasis on good food, good drink, and good cooking. Many Louisiana cooks have a wide assortment of crab recipes that derive from our state's rich mix of ethnic and racial diversity, including Cajun French. The best from Louisiana have been selected for this book. A few international crab recipes, such as Chinese, French, Italian, Caribbean, Mexican-American, Japanese, Thai, and Greek, have also been included.

Recipes for regional crab specialties in the United States also were tracked down and added to the collection. The Chesapeake Bay watermen were the first in our country to harvest and export hard and soft-shell blue crabs on a large scale. Consequently, that southern region has had a strong influence on crab cookery throughout the United States.

Probably the most popular crab dishes in the Chesapeake area today are crab cakes, Crabmeat Imperial, and steamed crabs spiced with Old Bay powder or something similar. South Carolina is famous for she-crab soup. Florida is known for its deviled crab, boiled blue crabs, and steamed or boiled stone crab claws eaten with a variety of sauces.

West Coast Americans eat Dungeness and Alaskan king crabs in a wide variety of ways, sometimes as fast-food, hot-crab sandwiches on sourdough bread or as crabburgers. San Francisco is noted for an Italian-inspired dish, Cioppino (pronounced "cha-PEE-no"), a hearty soup with crab and other seafood. Californians have developed elegant crab dishes that show Mexican and Oriental influences and that complement their good wines.

In Oregon, Native American, East Coast, and West Coast cooking influences have converged, resulting in an eclectic mix of cuisines. This is also true for Alaska, where there are dishes like king crab paella, pickled king crab legs, and king crabmeat and fruit salads that are divine.

Special thanks are owed to the following individuals who kindly helped in the research and/or who generously shared their favorite recipes. Their names will be given here, rather than in the text. Without the help of these good people, this book would not have been possible.

In Louisiana: Kent and Marian Burgess of Sid-Mar's Restaurant in Bucktown; Marie Windell, Sam Rabinowitz, Lambros G. Randis, Marie Mumme, Elinor S. Cohen, Marie R. Bloemer, Carole Grout, Joanne Moulton, Isaac Granderson, Theone Velez, Ruth Sogin, Ed Griffin; and, big sister, Carla Bayard.

In Mississippi: Niece Vicki Lynn Long and the Fayard and Ladner families.

In Florida: Cousin Barbara Touard Mills and Joe Mills, and Marie Holmes and Tom Thomas from the Florida Department of Agriculture and Consumer Service, Bureau of Seafood and Aquaculture. Thanks also go to the latter for permission to use the diagrams and the many recipes from their publications.

In Maryland: Bob and Betty Gray.

In South Carolina: Cousin Buddy Touard.

In Georgia: Aunt Helen Gravetti.

In Oregon: Cousin Anita Lewisohn Hamm, Vivian Wheeler, Jacque Heiden, Kathrine French, Neil T. Richmond, Al J. Didier, and Nick Furman, the Dungeness Crab Commissioner.

In Florence, Oregon: Joyce and George Mouzakis, Jeanne Condo (a transplanted Californian), Johnny Simmons and David Heckathorn, chefs at the International C-food Restaurant, Ted and Jan Weber of Weber's Fish House, Warner Pinkney of the Sportsman, Wayne at the Krab Kettle, and—last but not least—the following fishermen, sports crabbers, and tale-tellers: LaVell Cottam, Dannie Owens, David Howell, Tom Wilheight.

In Alaska: Cheryl G. Hull, publications specialist for the Alaska Department of Fish and Game, and that department for permission to use recipes from their cookbook.

Special thanks also go to Dr. Mike Moody of the Louisiana Cooperative Extension Service and to the Louisiana Seafood Promotion and Marketing Board for their assistance.

Two of my colleagues from the Department of Anthropology at the University of New Orleans, Malcolm Webb and Rick Shenkel, gave help pertaining to crabs in archeology.

On Becoming a Crab Lover
A Personal Introduction

Having grown up in New Orleans, I was exposed very early in life to the joys and terrors of opening, cracking, and picking boiled blue crabs. Sometimes I bloodied my fingers on their sharp shells or claws. Once, because there was no nutcracker on hand, I foolishly broke a tooth biting a crab claw instead of daintily cutting it open with a knife. That costly experience taught me an important anthropological lesson: never use a body part for a job that can be done by a tool!

Although my immediate family loved to eat boiled crabs, we never ate them at home because none of the men knew how or liked to cook. Louisiana "crab boils" take place outdoors and are traditionally conducted by men. That way, the cooking crabs, boiling in highly spiced water, won't heat and smell up the kitchen and entire house.

Instead of cooking at home, our family took the easy way out and went to one of the numerous seafood restaurants on the shores of Lake Pontchartrain, either in West End or in Little Woods. Our family's favorite place for boiled crabs was Bruning's Seafood Restaurant in West End, owned and operated by the same family for almost a hundred and fifty years. It and a few more like it are still out there.

These seafood eateries were large, wooden, one-story buildings sitting atop pilings over the murky, brackish lake waters. In the old days they were surrounded by screen porches where one could enjoy the lake breezes while picking crabs. Today's newer, air-conditioned versions are usually missing the screen porches but still afford good views of the lake with sailboats and speedboats going by and sea gulls flying overhead. Often one enters such establishments by way of a long and narrow wooden pier over the water. Boiled blue crabs were, and still are, sold by the dozen or half dozen. When they are boiled they turn a bright red-orange color. They arrive at the table arranged neatly on dark brown plastic trays, looking like they have been polished with oil. Nutcrackers are provided, in addition to knives and forks, to extract the crabmeat. Instead of bread, the crabs are served with saltine crackers and fresh lemon wedges and sometimes with a little paper cup containing horseradish. Usually on the table are bottles of catsup and Louisiana hot sauce—all the makings for a catsup-based cocktail sauce, if one wishes.

In the old days, the big tables sometimes were covered with newspaper before the crabs were served. When the heaping trays of well-seasoned, boiled crabs arrived, they were placed right in the middle where everyone could reach them. Afterward, cleaning up was simple. The impromptu newspaper tablecloth was rolled up with all the crab shells inside and tossed in the trash.

Eating dozens of boiled crabs always took our family lots and lots of time. We sat for what seemed like hours, laughing, eating, gossiping, people-watching, bird- and boat-watching, and enjoying one another's company over succulent morsels of crabmeat washed down with soft drinks, iced tea, or cold beer.

Afterwards, if we were still hungry, some of us would order a New Orleans specialty: battered and fried soft-shell crabs served on hot, buttered, toasted French bread—the famous soft-shell crab po-boy sandwich.

Even more fun than eating boiled crabs on a restaurant's screen porch over the lake was going crabbing. The most memorable crabbing trips took place during summer visits to Grandmother's home town, Bay St. Louis, Mississippi. We would pile in the family car and drive the sixty-odd miles to stay with Aunt Emma and Uncle Andrew Carver for a few days of fun in the sun.

The round drop nets we used to catch crabs were handmade by Uncle Andrew, an old sea-salted fisherman. He would crochet them with white parcel string. I can picture him now, sitting on a stool on his back porch, using both hands to crochet the nets while simultaneously smoking short, unfiltered cigarettes. He had a craggy, creased, outdoorsman's face that perpetually seemed in need of a shave. His fingers were gnarled and there was usually a twinkle in his blue eyes.

Besides blowing perfect smoke rings, Uncle Andrew could do something even more spectacular with a lighted cigarette. He could invert his lips and make the small cigarette butt disappear inside his mouth! Then he would imitate a dragon and exhale the smoke from his nostrils! Returning his lips to their normal position, he made the tiny little cigarette reappear, and, amazingly, he wasn't even burned! Uncle Andrew was a real character.

Most of the crabbing expeditions that I took part in were in the daytime, but it is well known in local folklore that the best time to catch blue crabs is at night when the moon is full. Uncle Andrew and his sons sometimes went crabbing then, but they left the kids at home.

To go crabbing we would walk the two blocks down to the narrow beach and then another block or so to a long wooden pier with high, splintery railings. The wood was always unpainted and had a pearly-gray color from exposure to the sun, wind, and salt. At the end of the pier was a large, roofed area with benches along the sides where one could sit to get out of the sun. There was also a stepladder going down into the warm, shallow, murky, gulf waters. The water is shallow near the beachfront in Bay St. Louis, and too close to the mouth of the Mississippi River to be clear blue-green and sparkling as it is farther east in Pensacola, Florida.

We almost always used fresh chicken necks for bait, because they were cheap and they worked very well with the blue crabs. The raw necks were secured with extra large safety pins to the string bottoms of the round, one-ring and two-ring drop nets. Three pieces of string were attached to the upper rim of each net. The ends of the three strings were tied together and attached to a rather long piece of thin rope that was wound around a flat piece of wood that would float if dropped over the side of the pier.

We usually took at least a dozen crab nets and several round wooden hampers on these official crabbing expeditions. The nets were spaced evenly down both sides of the long pier and tied to the railing. The grownups usually retreated to the benches and the shade at the end of the pier and let the kids run up and down pulling up the nets.

You had to pull fast, as fast as your hands could go, or else the tricky blue crabs would escape from the nets and splash back into the frothy gray-brown water. Although not hampered by conservation laws governing crab size, we nevertheless always tossed back the "babies." We wanted to catch fat crabs, those that were heavy with meat and orange fat.

Occasionally the children had crabbing adventures without adult supervision and real crabnets. The adults were glad to be rid of us for awhile, and the sport was fairly safe. All we needed was some string, raw bacon or chicken necks, and a hamper. With the raw bait tied securely to the end of the string, we would dangle it into the murky waters beneath the wooden piers and wait for a tug on the line. Then the fun and excitement would begin.

It was a combination of skill and luck to get the crabs up on the pier in the first place, because most of them dropped the bait as soon as they emerged from the water. But the greedy ones held on tight, and up they came. If the hamper was nearby it was fairly easy to plop them inside it. Otherwise, the crabs usually dropped down on the pier and began to scramble back toward the pier's edge and safety. This was when raw courage was useful to grab a crab or to step on it and stop its escape. Sturdy shoes were helpful for holding them down without getting toes pinched, but sandals were better suited to the summer heat. Sandals introduced an added element of danger, since little toes frequently extended over the edge, just where a crab claw might find it.

We said the crabs were running if they were plentiful and easy to catch. In such cases, we might fill the hampers in just an hour or so. When that happened, or when we were too hot, thirsty, and sunburned to stay out any longer, we went back to Aunt Emma's house. The crab boil took place soon thereafter, before the crabs died but after we had rested and cooled off. Uncle Andrew was usually in charge.

A huge aluminum cauldron was filled with salted water and commercially sold crab boil seasonings, plus other secret ingredients known only to Uncle Andrew. After this peppery witches' brew boiled for a while, the live crabs were tossed into the bubbling, boiling inferno. Sometimes we thought we could hear the crabs scream. Mostly we tried not to think about that part, and focused instead on the feast that was to come.

Sometimes Uncle Andrew also boiled small new potatoes and pieces of corn on the cob together with the crabs. The result was perfect. Uncle Andrew said it was even better when washed down with large quantities of ice-cold beer.

As a little girl I loved fried soft-shell crabs even better than boiled ones, despite an allergy. My eyes would get puffy and I broke out in hives every time I ate them. Mother would take me to the family pediatrician, Dr. Chapman, for a painful allergy shot. He once told her, "If you keep letting Mary Ethelyn eat those crabs you'll either cure her or kill her!" Obviously it's not so easy to kill an undaunted crab-lover like myself.

The Crab Lover's Book

Cooking and Cleaning Fresh Crabs

(or Choosing the Store-Bought Kind)

The British are noted animal rights advocates. Their attitude is clearly revealed in one English cookbook in which the author chastised fishermen for their cruelty in not quickly killing the crabs they caught. She thought it punishment most terrible to keep crabs alive artificially in small prisons where they fought and clawed at one another.

Furthermore, she thought it completely barbarous that the poor crabs were dumped alive into boiling water in order to be cooked for consumption. She suggested that all crab-pot men should first stun the crabs they caught with a mallet before dropping them into boiling water to cook. (Evidently she thought being bashed with a mallet was preferable to being boiled alive.)

The African Americans of South Carolina's coastal islands have the following retort to the above British attitude: "Crab got tuh walk een duh pot demself or day ain' wut."

The people of Louisiana agree with the latter sentiment.

Frank Davis, a noted New Orleans chef and cookbook author, says: "Crabs should not be purchased unless they are alive and kicking. I suggest that you discard all dead crabs prior to boiling, unless you caught them yourself and they died on ice."

Commercially Prepared Crabmeat

All of the recipes in this collection make use of cooked crabmeat, and any type of edible crabmeat can be used. The most common way to obtain this, in Louisiana, is to boil the crabs alive and then extract the meat.

If, however, you prefer to avoid this perhaps onerous, time-consuming, and somewhat arduous task, you can purchase cooked crabmeat, fresh or frozen. Canned crabmeat is the least tasty alternative and is not highly recommended, especially when other types are available.

Any type of commercially prepared, pre-cooked crabmeat can be used in the following recipes. When a recipe specifies a particular type of crabmeat, best results will be obtained when that recommendation is followed.

Always drain purchased crabmeat of all liquid and then carefully inspect by hand, removing tiny bits of shell or cartilage.

Meat From Blue Crabs

There are three grades of commercially produced meat from blue crabs. The most expensive is called **lump meat** and consists of solid, succulent chunks of white meat from the backfin of the crab. This type is used in recipes such as cocktails and salads when the finished appearance is very important. No substitutions should be made for this type. Lump meat can be presented simply; sautéed in butter or resting on a bed of lettuce with a salad dressing, it makes an elegant and tasty dish. In a lemon-butter sauce it is a wonderful topping for grilled or pan-fried fish, and mixed into a delicate cream sauce it is also excellent over veal or poultry.

White, special, or *flake meat* consists of small pieces of white meat from the rest of the body. This type is less expensive to purchase and is suitable for the bulk of the recipes that follow. This product is also ideal for basic crab dressing used for stuffing fish, shrimp, artichokes, and the like. A little flake meat added to seafood gumbo or chowder imparts the flavor and appeal of crab for a fraction of the cost of lump meat.

Claw meat is the meat picked from the blue crab's claws which is sometimes brownish in color. It should not be used in recipes where the final appearance is important. This meat stores better in the freezer than other crab meat. Claw meat can easily be used in place of flake meat in many recipes such as gumbo or crab dressing. Simply chop the meat into small pieces. Since its cost is lower than the other two types, it can be used for less expensive dishes with comparable taste.

Crab fingers or *cocktail fingers* consist of the blue crab's claw meat left intact on the claw with its surrounding shell removed. The claw provides a handy stem for the bite-sized morsel of meat. This "convenience food" is fast becoming a popular menu item. Crab fingers are an economical appetizer that come precooked. They can be marinated or fried and served with a variety of dips.

Meat From Other Varieties Of Crab

In today's world of rapid shipment of perishable foods, live crabs and fresh or frozen crabmeat from many kinds of crabs can be purchased almost everywhere. Live Dungeness crabs from Oregon are now sold in grocery stores and seafood markets throughout the country, whereas a few years ago, only live blue crabs were available.

In the Pacific Coast area, excellent fresh-picked Dungeness crabmeat is readily available in seafood markets in many inland towns and cities. It is usually sold in one grade only and consists of meat from the legs mixed together with body meat.

Whole fresh cooked Dungeness crabs can even be shipped in dry ice directly to one's doorstep from such seafood markets as Pike's Peak in Seattle.

If large chunks of crab leg meat are purchased for the following recipes that call for crabmeat, be sure to chop and flake the chunks so that the meat can be dispersed throughout the dish.

The meat from blue crabs is high in protein, rich in minerals, and relatively low in fat. However, dieters should be aware that, while crabs are lower in protein than shrimp, their fat content by weight is generally two times higher. The official statistics for blue crab are 78 calories for 3½ ounces of raw crabmeat and 60 to 75 milligrams of cholesterol per serving.

Imitation Crabmeat

Surimi, or imitation king crabmeat, is another option. This rather inexpensive product is a good substitute for persons on a low-calorie, low-cholesterol diet or those with allergies to shellfish. Made from pollock, a Pacific Ocean white fin fish (or from other, similar fish), it is best used in salads and those recipes that do not involve extensive cooking. Lengthy cooking at high temperature can cause the product to shred or become stringy and rubbery. The recipes in this collection have *not* been tested using this product; however, feel free to experiment if you are a frugal gourmet.

Boiled Crabs

Some people living along the Pacific Coast who enjoy sport crabbing like to boil Dungeness crabs in seawater in large pots or kettles, frequently right on the beach over a big fire made of driftwood. Seawater has the perfect salt content and is free for the taking. Many feel no need for sauces or condiments and believe that pepper or other spices overpower the wonderfully subtle and delicate flavor of freshly cooked Dungeness crab-meat.

After a long, fun day of crabbing, many native Oregonians like to have oceanside picnics. It's hard to beat the experience of eating good Dungeness crab while a Pacific sunset and pounding surf form the background. For most sport crabbers, crab fishing means fun, free food for the table, and a thrilling recreational experience.

Elsewhere, especially in Louisiana, people prefer to eat hot, peppery crabs that have been boiled in spiced and salted fresh-water. The Zatarain Food Company from New Orleans has, for over one hundred years, sold its famous crab boil seasoning, loose and in bags. Crab boil is an excellent mix of spices, seeds, peppercorns, and bay leaves. The small sacks are dropped directly into boiling, salted water, and the flavor goes through the sack and into the water. These handy bags hold all the little pieces of spices and leaves, eliminating the need for straining. Zatarain Liquid Crab Boil is also available. Directions for the suggested amounts of crab boil are printed on the containers. These condiments are easy to use and give an excellent, some-what spicy flavoring to crabmeat.

Other premixed spices are available for those who want less pepper. Oregon seafood markets like Webers' Fish House in Florence sell whole, boiled crabs that have been cooked in salted water and pickling spice. This is a commercially pro-duced condiment that generally contains cinnamon, allspice, mustard seed, coriander, bay leaves, ginger, chilies, cloves, black pepper, mace, and cardamom and is also used for the making of sweet pickles. Jan Weber says that when fresh garlic is in season and inexpensive, she adds a few cloves to each pot for extra flavor.

The following recipe was used by Louisiana and Gulf Coast Creoles in the days before Zatarain's Crab Boil was available. It is included for those who live in places where such condiments are not available, or who want to try a Creole crab boil.

Creole Boiled Crabs For Two

Large pot of water
Salt sufficient to make a brine
3 stalks of celery and the tops
2 dozen allspice
4 sprigs thyme
4 sprigs chives
1 lemon, sliced
1 onion, sliced
4 sprigs sweet basil
4 sprigs marjoram
3 leaves mace
3 bay leaves
1 red pepper pod
Cayenne pepper to taste
1 dozen live blue crabs

The rule of thumb in cooking boiled blue crabs is to cook from four to six per person. Buy large crabs, remembering that the livelier they are the better. The crabs must be alive when put into the pot. Prepare a large pot with water enough to cover the crabs and add salt, about ¼ cup per quart of water, or enough to make a brine. Add all the seasonings and boil for about fifteen minutes. Put in the live crabs and let them boil rapidly for about ten minutes, or until the shells are a bright red. Turn off the heat. Do not boil longer than this or the crabs will become watery. Let them cool a little in their own water and then take them out.

Boiling Crabs the Kent Burgess Way

Kent Burgess and his family own and operate a successful seafood restaurant called Sid-Mar's in Bucktown, a small fishing village on the south shore of Lake Pontchartrain in Metairie,

Louisiana. Their restaurant is one of the old-fashioned types with a screen porch on two sides to catch lake breezes and a view of the shrimp boats tied to the docks. Kent has his own version of the best way to cook perfect boiled blue crabs. "Anybody can boil crabs, but they're not going to come out the same. I always use more spices than what you're supposed to put in," he says, referring to the spices sold commercially for boiled crabs.

The critical step in the Burgess method is first to stun the crabs by refrigerating them alive overnight or to chill them in ice water if boiling is to be immediate. "Stunned crabs are less likely to kick off their claws when they hit the boiling water," Burgess explains. Another important step is to use enough seasoning and then let the crabs soak in the seasoning after they cook. This means dumping them in ice to stop the cooking and giving them time to absorb the cayenne pepper, garlic, lemon juice, and salt that Burgess adds to the crab boil spices.

Burgess says some crab lovers he knows come in every Friday night and can eat two and a half dozen crabs! He adds that some people won't eat anything but females and others prefer males. The reason for the preference is the fat.

"Everyone likes fat crabs, but they don't always agree on what fat means," he says. "To some it means the yellow fat more common in females or the orange eggs found in some females. Real boiled crab connoisseurs spread the fat and eggs on crackers to go along with their crabmeat. Other people define fat crabs as the heavy, full ones, usually the males. They are the ones that have more meat, but less yellow fat. So when our customers ask for fat crabs, we ask them if they want males or females."

Louisiana-Style Spicy Boiled Crabs

The following recipe can be used to boil from 2½ to 3 dozen small to medium-sized blue crabs. Use a 10-gallon pot half full of water. To this add:

2 heads garlic, sliced in half

6 lemons, halved

6 bay leaves, fresh (if available)

36 ounces of salt

3 onions, cut in pieces

1 stalk of chopped celery

½ cup Liquid Crab Boil

2 Tbls. cayenne pepper

If available, add 1 Tbl. Cracked Crab Boil (a commercially
produced powder)

Add ingredients to the cold water, squeezing the lemon halves to release the juice. Bring the water and spices to a full boil. Cover the pot for about 10 minutes and reduce the heat to a full simmer. When the seasonings are cooked in, add the live (but stunned) crabs. Replace the lid and wait for the water to come back to a full boil. When it does, begin to time the cooking process, about 8 minutes. Do not overcook or the crabmeat will have a mushy texture. Take the pot off the fire, dump in about ½ bag of crushed ice and let the crabs soak in the seasonings for another 15 to 45 minutes. Check on the seasonings after the first 15 minutes, adding more if needed, according to taste. The longer the crabs soak, the more flavor they absorb. NOTE: If the cooking is being done outdoors on a propane gas burner, the water will boil more quickly (the fire is hotter than on a gas stove). You may need to lower the cooking time to from 5 to 8 minutes.

Simmered Crabs

Some folks prefer to cook with crabmeat that has not been as highly seasoned as in the previous recipes. If this applies to you, then you may want to simmer or steam your crabs.

To simmer the crabs, first purge them in cold, salty water for 20 minutes. Rinse. Place 24 live hard-shell blue crabs in 6 quarts boiling water that contains ⅓ cup salt and 3–6 halved lemons. Cover the pot and return the water to the boiling point. Reduce the heat and simmer for 12 to 15 minutes. Drain and rinse in cold water. Serve hot or cold.

Crabs may also be cleaned before cooking, as in the Buddy Touard approach, and only the claws and inner skeleton or pod which contains the white body meat cooked. However, the cooking time should be reduced to 5 to 7 minutes.

Chesapeake Bay Steamed Blue Crabs

Some crab lovers from the East Coast and the southeastern parts of the United States like to steam blue crabs using a seasoning that was specifically devised for this purpose: Old Bay Seasoning. It is a mixture of celery salt, pepper, dry mustard, pimiento, cloves, laurel leaves, mace, cardamom, ginger, cassia, and paprika. Sold all over the country in a bright yellow-and-blue can, it is an excellent seasoning for many seafood dishes, as well as for chicken and beef. The following recipe is specifically developed for use with Old Bay.

Water and white vinegar
12 blue crabs
3 Tbls. salt
2½ Tbls. Old Bay powder

Use a pot that has a raised rack that is at least 2 inches high. Add equal amounts of white vinegar and water (some people substitute beer or part beer and part water) to just below the level of the rack. Layer the crabs. Sprinkle some on each layer. Mix salt and Old Bay powder together. Cover and steam the crabs until they are bright red.

Oregon Coast Seaweed-Wrapped Steamed Crabs

If you go crabbing in areas where seaweed is plentiful, you might want to try another tasty way to steam crabs. David Heckathorn, a native Oregonian and seafood chef, prefers to steam Dungeness crabs this way. He and his friends often go crabbing along the rocky Pacific shoreline. As they gather crabs, they also gather fresh seaweed from the beach. When enough crabs for the evening's meal have been caught, they build a large fire and place a metal cooking rack over it. When the coals are glowing, they place the crabs, individually wrapped in seaweed, around the edge of the fire or on the "cool end of the grill." It is only necessary to turn the crabs over once. When they are finished, they are flavored with a delicious taste of sea salt and seaweed.

How To Eat Hard-Boiled Blue Crabs

A boiled, steamed, or simmered crab is a difficult and potentially dangerous food item that must be approached with skill and care; in fact, there is a science to eating them.

The elegant Creoles of nineteenth-century New Orleans devised the following directions in order to eat blue crabs delicately, without using the fingers:

> If the crabs are boiled and served whole, then the shell and claws should be gently cracked in the kitchen before being brought to the table. By a skillful manipulation of the knife and fork, remove the apron, the small loose shell running to a point about the middle of the under shell. Then cut the crab claws off, still using the knife and fork. Last, cut the crab into two halves, and these again in two. Using a small fork, daintily extract the meat from each quarter.

The above method of eating boiled crabs is probably still in use among the more genteel members of New Orleans high society, although it appears to be in decline.

For today's average boiled crab consumer, the necessary tools are a pair of hands and a small knife. Simply follow the steps given here, and look at the accompanying illustrations.

1. With the crab upside down, grasp the legs on one side firmly with one hand, and with the other hand lift the flap (apron), pull back and down to remove the top shell.

2. Turn the crab right side up, remove the gills and wash out the intestines and spongy material.

3. With a twisting motion, pull the legs loose from the body. Remove any meat which adheres to the legs. Break off the claws.

4. Slice off the top of the inner skeleton and remove all exposed meat on this slice.

5. At the back of the crab on each side lies a large lump of meat. With a very careful U-shaped motion of the knife, remove this back fin lump.

6. Remove the white flake meat from the other pockets with the point of the knife.

7. Crack the claw shell and remove the shell along with the moveable pincer. This will expose the claw meat and, if meat is left attached to the remaining pincer, will make a delicious "crab finger" hors d'oeuvre. Or the dark meat can be removed and used in soups, casseroles or salads.

Hint: both the yellow fat found inside blue crabs and the orange eggs found inside females are delicious and should not be ignored. Try it, you'll like it! Scoop the fat out with your fingers, or be more sophisticated and use a knife to spread it on a cracker. This makes a wonderful impromptu hors d'oeuvre.

How to Cook and Clean Dungeness Crabs

According to the Oregon Dungeness Crab Commission, the best way to cook Dungeness crabs is to place them live in boiling, salted water. When the water begins to reboil, cook them for 18 to 20 minutes. The crabs will turn bright orange. Immerse them in cold water to cool before cleaning.

For cleaning, it is best to refrigerate your whole-cooked crabs until ready to eat. Then observe the diagrams, and follow these simple steps:

1. To remove back, hold base of the crab with one hand, place thumb under shell at mid-point, and pull off the shell.
2. The leaf-like gills are now exposed. Gently scrape them away with your thumb or a spoon edge.
3. Wash away the viscera (if desired) under a heavy stream of cold water.

1

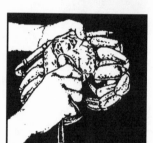

2

Cleaning Crabs Before Cooking

In my early experiences boiling blue crabs in Louisiana and Mississippi, we never cleaned them before cooking. We wanted the crabs to go into the pot kicking and showing signs of life.

On the other hand, my first cousin Buddy Touard, who grew up in Atlanta, Georgia, learned another approach. He says that the secret to good boiled crabs is to clean them *before* they are cooked. I myself have reservations about getting up close and personal with a dozen or so angry blue crabs, but in case you are of the Buddy Touard school of thought, the following information is provided for you. I accept no responsibility, however, for nicks and scrapes from agitated blue or other crabs. Before you begin, put on heavy gloves.

3

1. Stun the crabs by immersing them in ice water for fifteen minutes.
2. Remove the carapace or back of the crab by forcing the edge of the shell against any solid object.
3. Break the crab in two by folding it like a book—first up and then down.
4. Shake out the viscera from each half.
5. Pull off the gill filaments. Nothing remains but shell and edible meat.

If this method is used, the cooking time will be greatly reduced.

Grilled Crabs

Grilling or barbecuing crabs is popular in various parts of the world including Greece. This process gives the crabmeat a completely different texture and flavor.

Start with large, live crabs. Clean them according to the Buddy Touard method just described. To make a Greek marinade, combine olive oil, lemon juice, fresh minced garlic, bay leaf, oregano, salt, and pepper (if you like more pepper, add a few drops of Tabasco sauce). Marinate the cleaned, raw crab quarters in the refrigerator for at least 6 hours before cooking.

To grill, place crabs directly on the cooking rack, about 6 inches above the hot coals. Cover and cook for about 20 minutes, or until the meat comes easily out of the shell.

Appetizers & More

Crab Facts

Crab Festivals

Indian Myths

Joyce's Crab Cocktail Sauce

1 cup mayonnaise
4 drops Tabasco sauce
1 tsp. onion powder
1 tsp. dried garlic
½ cup Zatarain's Creole mustard*

Mix all ingredients together and chill for about an hour to set the flavors. Serve atop lump crabmeat in large cocktail glasses.

*Creole Mustard is a unique product made by Zatarain's, Inc. of New Orleans. This company has been in the food business since 1889. Their Creole Mustard has no exact substitute, but the listed ingredients on the bottle are "ground mustard seed, distilled vinegar, and salt with algin derivative added."

Crab Facts

Crabs first appear in the fossil record early in the Jurassic period of the Mesozoic, nearly 200 million years ago. There are some 4,500 species of identified and described crabs in the world, many of which are edible. Crabs are found on every continent. They contribute to human welfare both directly as food for people and indirectly as food for fishes and other animals.

In the scientific world, crabs are classified as crustaceans. What a perfect label for creatures that look like living, miniature, armored tanks! Consider the bravery of the first humans who decided hundreds of thousands of years ago that crabs might be good to eat, because they most definitely don't look like anything edible.

The tasty and good-to-eat crustaceans are the decapods, the ten-legged ones such as lobsters, shrimp, and crabs. Other crustaceans include wood lice, barnacles, and water fleas. (Although these might be tasty when well prepared, they don't sound like anything we would want to try any time soon.)

The thousands of known living crab species exist in an incredibly wide range of habitats: from the tops to the bottoms of seas, on tropical sandy beaches and muddy shores, in freshwater rivers, estuaries, and lakes (a few can be found in lakes at altitudes of 2,100 meters). Some crabs live on land in damp habitats; some live on or in the bodies of other organisms. Crabs are even found living underground! One brave species manages to live in the hellish world beneath the earth's crust, near volcanic vents.

The crab body is a fusion of the head and the thorax and is covered by a hard carapace. The crab abdomen (corresponding to what gourmets call the tail of the lobster) is reduced to a thin, flat plate, tucked forward out of sight below the body. Hence the scientific name for true crabs is Brachyura, meaning shortailed crabs.

The crab body is covered by a hard exoskeleton that offers protection but limits growth. Periodically, a crab seeks a sheltered hiding place, reabsorbs

Crab Cocktail Sauce

1 cup mayonnaise
½ tsp. Worcestershire sauce
1 tsp. lemon juice
½ tsp. Tabasco sauce
1 tsp. curry powder
¼ cup chili sauce
½ tsp. minced onion
Salt and pepper to taste

Mix well and keep in the refrigerator until ready to serve.

Traditional Crab Cocktail Sauce

½ cup tomato catsup
10 drops Tabasco sauce
3 Tbls. cider vinegar or lemon juice
Salt and pepper to taste

Mix and let stand at least two hours. To vary, add 1 teaspoon each of chopped parsley, chopped chives, and horseradish, and season with prepared mustard and Worcestershire to taste. Or add finely chopped celery or parsley.

Herb and Mayonnaise Crab Cocktail Sauce

1 cup mayonnaise
½ tsp. capers, drained
2 tsp. fresh basil, chopped
2 tsp. fresh dill, chopped
2 green onions, chopped
2 drops Tabasco sauce

Blend all the ingredients together and chill.

Chinese Ginger Sauce for Steamed Crabs

Cook a suitable number of crabs for each person. Transfer steamed (or boiled, etc.) crabs to a serving platter and serve hot with the ginger sauce.

Sauce
3 tsp. chopped fresh ginger*
4 tsp. sugar
3 tsp. soy sauce
3 tsp. red wine vinegar

Combine all ingredients and stir to blend well. Place in a small, deep dish, suitable for dipping the crabmeat into. Prepare one sauce recipe per person.

*Fresh ginger root can be purchased at many grocery stores and/or at Chinese markets.

Marinated Crab Claws

1 pound blue crab claws, cracked and partly peeled
1 stalk celery, minced
¼ cup minced green onions
¼ cup minced parsley
1 clove garlic, minced
2 Tbls. tarragon vinegar
¼ cup fresh lemon juice
¼ cup virgin olive oil
½ cup water
¼ cup Wishbone Italian salad dressing*
Pinch of oregano
Dash of Worcestershire sauce

Mix all the ingredients except crab claws in a large bowl and chill for at least 8 hours. Add the crab claws and marinate for another 4 hours in the refrigerator.

some materials from its exoskeleton, then splits the remaining shell and crawls or wriggles out of it. In a short time the new exoskeleton, already partly formed inside the old shell but still thin and soft, thickens and hardens. Before it does this, however, the crab absorbs considerable water and expands to a size larger than before the molt.

Crabs have five pairs of walking legs, the first of which are modified as chelipeds (pincers or claws). Any crab whose leg becomes trapped or is gripped by a predator can escape by quickly shedding the limb and running away. Locomotory effectiveness is scarcely affected by the loss. This makes crabs very hard to catch by one appendage.

The shape of the crab is the ultimate design for efficient crustacean walking. The crab's abdomen and center of gravity is located directly over its walking legs. This makes movement, even the curious sideways gait, very efficient and rapid.

The Greek philosopher Aristotle was so interested in the variety and strange modes of life of this creature that he wrote the first short essay on crabs. It focused on the tiny oyster crab (*Pinnoteres pisun*), which has a diameter of one or two centimeters. The female spends her entire life living inside an inhabited mussel shell while the male oyster crabs are freeliving. These female squatters remain true to their mussels and feed from the surplus food their hosts waft by. When the breeding season comes around, the females abandon the comforts of home to go out and meet males. Afterwards, the mothers-to-be return to the protection of their shelled mussel hosts.

Truth is always stranger than fiction. The giant heavenly crab of Greek mythology and the zodiac has an earthly counterpart in the Japanese spider crab (*Macrocheir kaempferi*). The largest of all crustaceans, it can measure 26.5 feet between the tips of its legs when they are splayed out on either side of its body. The long claws may be ten feet apart when held in an offensive posture. Surprisingly, the body is relatively small, only eighteen inches in length and twelve inches wide. Imag-

*This recipe works best with Wishbone brand Italian dressing; however, if it is unavailable, substitute your favorite brand.

Fried Crab Claws

Crab claws, cracked and peeled
Eggs, beaten
Self-rising flour
Oil for frying

Dip the cracked and peeled crab claws in the beaten eggs, then in the flour, then back in the egg, then back in the flour. Fry in hot oil until golden brown. Serve with cocktail sauce.

Florida Stone Crab Claws with Mustard Sauce

6–8 stone crab claws, cooked
½ cup dairy sour cream
1½ Tbls. prepared mustard
2 Tbls. melted butter
½ tsp. parsley flakes
⅛ tsp. salt

The crab claws may be served cold or steamed just a bit to re-heat them (they are sold fully cooked). To prepare the sauce, combine all the ingredients in a small saucepan. Heat at a very low temperature until just warm, stirring occasionally. DO NOT BOIL. Makes about ⅔ cup of sauce. (Recipe courtesy of the Florida Department of Agriculture and Consumer Services, Bureau of Seafood and Aquaculture.)

Louisiana Marinated Boiled Crabs

2 dozen boiled blue crabs
1 cup olive oil
1 cup Italian salad dressing
⅓ cup wine vinegar
⅔ cup chopped green onions
½ cup chopped celery
½ cup chopped green olives
4 garlic cloves, minced
1 tsp. Tabasco sauce
Salt and pepper to taste

Clean the crabs and cut in half, setting the claws aside. Place in a large, covered bowl. Mix the remaining ingredients and pour over the crab halves and claws; stir to coat with the seasoning. Marinate in the refrigerator for at least 12 hours.

Crab Canapés

1 Tbls. butter
2 Tbls. flour
2 Tbls. grated Parmesan cheese
¾ cup light cream
½ cup crabmeat
Salt and pepper to taste
Dash of garlic powder
1 egg yolk
2 Tbls. dry sherry
50 packaged canapé shells

Melt the butter. With the heat on low, add the flour gradually and stir with a whisk until smooth. Add the cheese and the cream and cook until thick, stirring constantly. Remove from the heat and stir in the crabmeat and seasonings. Beat the

ine the feast one could have with the meat from just one of these giant claws!

These crab monsters are found well off the southeast coast of Japan, where they live on sandy or muddy bottoms. On land they have very poor balance, so they usually stay in the sea. They are used for food but are quite costly. They are harvested with extreme caution since their nippers are quite dangerous to the Nipponese.

On the other side of the world there lives another fairly large crab, the Caribbean land crab (*Cardisoma guanhume*), whose shell diameter reaches fifteen centimeters. With their large defensive pincers they look very dangerous, but they often become quite tame when cared for by people. Some of these crab pets take fruit from their owner's hands! Considered a delicacy in local markets, they are very hard to catch because of their excellent vision and quick response to ground vibrations. Mating takes place underground, and the expectant females migrate to the sea in large numbers at the time of the full moon and deposit their well-developed larvae there at the time of the spring tides.

The spider crabs (family Majidae), include the decorator crabs such as *Loxorhynchus* and *Scyra*. These curious creatures disguise themselves from predators by attaching bits of sponges, hydroids, algae, and even tiny rocks to their shells. Some are true works of art.

An Indo-Pacific crab (*Lybia tesselata*) demonstrates an amazing behavior found among the crabs. It lives on coral reefs, and when danger threatens it picks up a stinging sea anemone in each pincer and stretches these toward the enemy! This defense posture is really a modification of a very basic and primitive threat gesture. Even blue crabs will raise their pincers toward a human enemy when on land and frightened.

Without a doubt the most fascinating crabs of all are the romantic fiddler crabs of Central America, a group well known for their conspicuous courtship behavior. For the Coclé people who lived in Panama between A.D. 500 and 1000, fiddler crabs were symbols of earthly love and fertility. Coclé pottery was decorated with especially beautiful stylized fiddler crab designs in red, black, and white.

egg yolk with the sherry and add to the crabmeat mixture. Spoon into the canapé shells and broil under medium heat for 2 or 3 minutes, until golden brown.

English High Tea Crabmeat Spread

1 pound crabmeat, chopped
1 cup Cheddar cheese, grated
⅓ cup mayonnaise
2 green onions, finely chopped

Mix all ingredients together. Spread on toast rounds, triangles, or crackers. Heat 5 to 10 minutes at 400° until hot and bubbly. Serve hot with tea and other teatime treats.

English Silk Stocking Crabmeat Spread

1 cup crabmeat, chopped
1 cup minced celery
1 tsp. lemon juice
Salt and pepper to taste
1 tsp. minced pimento (optional)
Mayonnaise to moisten

Combine everything and chill. Make dainty sandwiches with white bread, crusts removed. Slice sandwiches into triangles. Serve with other teatime treats.

Crab Dip

1 small onion, minced
2 Tbls. minced green pepper
2 Tbls. minced green onions

¼ pound butter
1 8-ounce package cream cheese
1 pound crabmeat
Few drops of Tabasco sauce
Cayenne pepper, to taste

Sauté onion, green pepper and green onions in two table-spoons of the butter; set aside. In a double boiler, melt cream cheese and remaining butter; blend well. Add crabmeat, seasonings and vegetables. Serve in a chafing dish with melba toast.

Spicy Cajun Crab Spread

1 pound crabmeat
1 package Italian salad dressing mix
1 cup dairy sour cream
½ cup mayonnaise
1 Tbls. Creole mustard
Chopped parsley (garnish)

Combine first five ingredients; chill several hours. Garnish with parsley. Serve with crackers, chips, or raw vegetables such as broccoli, carrot sticks, and cauliflower. Makes about 3 cups of spread.

Louisiana Crab Dip for a Large Party

¾ cup margarine
2 onions, minced
2 stalks celery, minced
3 Tbls. minced parsley
3 pounds crabmeat
1 large can evaporated milk

These amazing tropical shore-dwelling fiddler crabs have highly developed strands of sense cells in their body joints that function as vibration receptors. Consequently, a true communications system—a "tapping code"—has evolved. There is a fiddler crab Morse code used in nighttime courtship rituals when the females are sent love messages in the dark. With his large pincer, the male fiddler taps signals on the ground in a rhythmic series that says to nearby females, "Here I am, come and mate with me!"

The singing fiddler crab (*Uca musica*) is able to produce melodic sounds by rubbing parts of his body together. Still another, because of his dancing and waving movements, is named after the Greek muse of dance and is known as the Terpsichore fiddler crab (*Uca terpsichore*).

The daytime courtship of the colorful fiddler crabs is an amazing spectacle to observe. The American naturalist William Beebe said it was hard to consider them with scientific objectivity just because they had ten legs instead of two and a hard shell instead of an internal skeleton. As he learned about their various personalities, he came to think such physical features were unimportant.

Beebe took part in the thirty-eighth expedition of the Department of Tropical Research of the New York Zoological Society in 1937–38, which did field research in the Bahía Honda area of Panama. He described the amorous fiddler crab behavior from his unique perspective:

We observed an especially handsome emerald fiddler crab. He strutted in his finest colors and had tried for at least an hour to attract the attention of a little gray female about 10 centimeters away, but without success. He stopped his show for only very short feeding breaks, but she seemed to be ignoring him, improving her burrow, feeding greedily, and not deigning him a glance.

Finally, she stopped eating and appeared to be noticing him for the first time. This gave him a little encouragement, and his dancing became more lively; he swung his huge purple pincer up and down like a madman, and, while raising it proudly, performed curious drag-

2 pounds Velveeta cheese, cubed
½ tsp. garlic powder
1 can cream of mushroom soup
Salt and cayenne pepper to taste
Plain breadcrumbs

Melt margarine in a large, heavy pot; add the onions and celery. Cook with lid on pot over low heat for 20 minutes, stirring occasionally to keep vegetables from sticking and burning. Add parsley, crabmeat, evaporated milk, cheese, garlic powder, and mushroom soup. Cook about 20 minutes over a very low heat, still stirring occasionally. Add salt and pepper to taste. If the dip is watery, add breadcrumbs to thicken, if desired. Cook about another 15 minutes. Makes more than a gallon.

Creole Crab Dip with Mushrooms

1 stick margarine
1 large onion, chopped
1 can cream of mushroom soup
1 3–ounce package cream cheese
1 pound crabmeat
3–4 drops Tabasco sauce

Sauté onion in margarine. Add mushroom soup and cream cheese. Heat over low heat, stirring constantly, until well blended. Add crabmeat and Tabasco sauce; stir until well mixed. Serve in chafing dish with crackers or chips or in miniature pastry shells.

Florida Hot Crab Dip

3 8-ounce package cream cheese
3 cans crabmeat
2 tsp. dry mustard
$1/2$ tsp. garlic salt
1 tsp. fresh lemon juice
$1/2$ cup mayonnaise
$1/2$ tsp. seasoned salt
$1/4$ cup sherry

Melt the cream cheese in the top of a double boiler. Add the remaining ingredients, and mix well. Put the mixture in a chafing dish and serve warm with toasted triangles of thinly sliced white bread.

Microwave Crab Dip

The following recipe should be cooked in a 3-quart casserole dish.

$1/2$ cup margarine
1 cup minced onions
1 stalk celery, minced
1 Tbls. minced parsley
$1/2$ pound Velveeta cheese, cubed
$1/2$ cup evaporated milk
$1/3$ cup cream of mushroom soup, undiluted
$1/4$ tsp. garlic powder
$1/8$ tsp. thyme
$1/4$ tsp. cayenne pepper
1 pound crabmeat
$1/2$ cup seasoned bread crumbs

ging movements of his eight green legs. The female raised herself and approached a few centimeters nearer, stopping along the way for a little refreshment. The admirer danced faster and faster, and finally brought her completely under his spell. Almost hypnotized, she watched him from about 2.5 centimeters away.

Now the character of his dance changed and he slowly turned round like a mannequin under her gaze so that she could first admire his shiny green back and then his purple pincers. Finally, she approached within reach and he stroked her legs gently with his own; she did the same. They separated for a moment, and he danced a happy jig before dashing into his burrow. His shining pincer was the last to disappear, with a final irresistible wave. The female followed without hesitation.

Among these amorous fiddler crabs, each species has a unique courtship dance. Naturalists tell us that the dances are as different as the rhumba is from the waltz. One crab species even seems to have invented a crab jitterbug!

There is an astrological association of the crab with the moon that appears to have a basis in scientific fact. With their highly developed compound eyes, crabs use the signals of the height and movement of the moon to orient themselves within their environments. The position of the moon directs them to move toward their feeding grounds and toward their original sea habitat, where they release their larvae.

Crab courtship, beside being restricted to certain times of the year, is also governed by the phases of the moon. Science explains that the larvae's release (and a better distribution of the larvae) occurs at high tide. Human (crab) lovers know that nights of the full moon are very romantic.

Is crabmeat an aphrodisiac? In the folklore of Western Civilization, all seafood is credited with this quality. This is because the ancient Greeks believed that Aphrodite, the goddess of love and beauty, was created from seafoam. Known also as Venus and the evening star, she rises nightly from the sea waters and glows radiantly in the western sky. Since the primeval sea was the source of all life, for many folk seafood is sex food.

Melt the margarine in the 3-quart casserole on HIGH for 1 minute. Add onions, celery and parsley. Microwave on HIGH for 5 minutes. Stir in cheese, milk, mushroom soup, garlic powder, thyme and cayenne pepper. Fold in crabmeat gently. Microwave on HIGH for 5 minutes, stirring once. Stir in enough bread crumbs for desired thickness.

King Crab Avocado Dip

1 6–8 ounce package frozen Alaska king crabmeat
1 large avocado
1 Tbls. lemon juice
1 Tbls. grated onion
1 tsp. Worcestershire sauce
¼ tsp. salt
1 8-ounce package cream cheese, softened
¼ cup dairy sour cream

Thaw, drain, and slice crab. In blender combine avocado, lemon juice, onion, Worcestershire sauce, and salt; blend until smooth. Add cream cheese and sour cream; blend well. Fold in crab. Cover and chill. Serve with crisp vegetables or potato chips. Makes 2 cups dip. (Recipe courtesy Alaska Department of Fish and Game.)

Microwave Crab Puffs

1 pound crabmeat
2 cups mayonnaise
Juice of small lemon
¼ tsp. salt
¼ tsp. cayenne pepper
3 egg whites
Triscuits or melba rounds

Combine crabmeat with mayonnaise. Add lemon juice, salt, and pepper. Beat egg whites until stiff and fold into crab mixture. Place one heaping teaspoon of crab mixture on each Triscuit or melba round. Arrange 12 on a paper plate (use 2 plates if thin). Microwave on HIGH for 1 minute 30 seconds per plate. Serve warm.

Louisiana Crab Party Pies

4 Tbls. butter
¾ cup chopped onions
¾ cup green pepper, chopped
2 garlic cloves, minced
½ pound crabmeat
1 small jar pimentos, minced
1 Tbls. dry sherry
1 tsp. salt
1 tsp. black pepper
1 tsp. Cayenne pepper
Cheese sauce
2 dozen bite-size pie shells, baked

Melt butter and sauté onion, chopped green pepper, and garlic until wilted. Add the crabmeat, pimentos, sherry, seasonings, and cheese sauce. Cook over low heat for 10 minutes. Pour into baked pie shells.

Cheese Sauce
2 Tbls. butter
2 Tbls. flour
1 cup milk
5 slices of American cheese, cut into small pieces
¼ tsp. salt

Then there is that astrological association of the crab with motherhood. As it turns out, some crab mothers-to-be do exhibit maternal behaviour. They attach their fertilized eggs to their own bodies and travel great distances with these egg packets. Some even carry their prodigy until the larval development has progressed to a relatively advanced level. So who says that astrology is only pseudo-science?

Archaeologists tell us that crab-loving humans have been eating crabs for as long as they could manage to catch them. At first they were eaten raw, and some people still like them that way. After fire was domesticated about five hundred thousand years ago, crab cuisine began. That makes for lots of time and lots of places for crab recipes to have developed.

Crab Festivals
The town of Crisfield, Maryland, which calls itself the "Blue Crabbing Capital of the World," annually hosts the Annual Hard Crab Derby and Fair on the Labor Day weekend. Started back in 1947, the races

became so successful that by 1973, a thirty-five-hundred-seat Crab Bowl was built near the Somers Cove Marina. Spectators can watch the races and other attractions in style and comfort.

Another main feature of the derby is the crab-picking contest, in which seasoned professionals compete for prize money and recognition. The contestants are generally women and girls employed in the Chesapeake crab houses that cook and process blue crab meat. These experts regularly pick as much as three or four pounds of meat in the fifteen-minute race. Since the average blue crab yield is only .14 of whole crab weight, this means that the winners are cleaning close to two crabs each minute.

During the three days of the Crisfield hard crab derby, there are fireworks, parades, beauty contests for the selection of Miss and Little Miss Crustacean, and country music concerts featuring singers such as Tammy Wynette. Food specialties include steamed crabs and barbecued chicken cooked over open pits.

The derby begins with tugs

Melt the butter; add the flour and milk and cook over a low heat until thick, stirring constantly. Add the cheese and salt; stir until melted.

Louisiana Crabmeat Napoleons

1 pound crabmeat
1½ cups béarnaise sauce
1 pound phyllo dough, frozen
½ cup butter, melted
½ cup seasoned bread crumbs
Ice water

Preheat the oven to 400°. Lightly grease a baking sheet. Combine the crabmeat and béarnaise sauce and set aside. Place first leaf of phyllo dough on baking sheet and brush with melted butter and sprinkle with bread crumbs. Repeat this process with 7 to 10 more leaves. Spread the crab mixture evenly over the last leaf. Begin layering the phyllo as before on top of crab mixture. Pile phyllo, butter, and bread crumbs 7 to 10 leaves high. Mold sides shut with ice water. Score the top in a diamond design to serve 24. If serving as a main dish, score 6 to 8 pieces. Brush top with remaining butter and bake in the middle of the oven for 25 to 30 minutes or until top is golden brown. Serve with additional sauce, in a serving dish.

Béarnaise Sauce
1 Tbls. butter, melted
1 Tbls. flour
1 Tbls. white wine
1 Tbls. chicken broth
6 green onions, chopped
½ clove of garlic, minced
Salt and black pepper to taste
¼ tsp. nutmeg, grated

¼ cup vinegar
Juice of ½ lemon
4 egg yolks, beaten well

In a saucepan over a low heat, add the flour to the butter and stir well. Add the wine and chicken broth and stir well. Add the green onions and garlic and continue to stir. Add the salt, pepper, nutmeg, vinegar, and lemon juice, stirring constantly. When the sauce has thickened, remove the saucepan from the fire and add the egg yolks, stirring constantly, until quite thick.

Florida Blue Crab Pâté

1 cup cold water
1 tsp. salt
1 package unflavored gelatin
1 pound crabmeat
1 cup mayonnaise
¼ cup minced green onions
1 tsp. dry mustard
Leaf lettuce as garnish

In small pot, combine water and salt. Soften gelatin in cold salted water for 4 minutes. Stir over low heat 1 or 2 minutes to dissolve. Cool slightly. Divide crabmeat into two equal portions. In blender or food processor, puree one of the crab portions with mayonnaise, green onions, and mustard. Add gelatin mixture. Process 2 seconds more or until blended. Gently fold in the remaining crabmeat. Pour into a well-greased 1-quart mold. Chill until firm, either several hours or overnight. Unmold onto the lettuce. Serve with warm French bread. (Recipe courtesy of the Florida Department of Agriculture and Consumer Services, Bureau of Seafood and Aquaculture.)

of war, greased pig runs, and log-sawing contests. Next are the crab-picking contests and boat-docking competitions, followed by contests to choose the World's Crabbiest Boss.

Of course, the biggest event of the fair is the derby itself, which features several heats with forty crabs, each bearing its number handpainted on top of its shell. The crabs are given fanciful names such as Spitfire or Lazy Boy and their own starting boxes. Heat winners compete in the final race in an effort to win a trophy for the lucky owner.

One main race was not enough, so the derby was expanded to include the Governor's Cup, in which each crab represents a state. Inland states have proxy blue crabs, which are given humorous names such as "Miss Shy Anne" for the state of Wyoming. Coastal states can enter any species of market crab regularly found in their waters.

It was logical for Crisfield to have a crab derby since it is said to be one of the richest centers of oral tradition in the United States. Down at the county dock, under a shade roof where you can watch the workboats come and go, there is a well-worn seat known to all as the "liar's bench." It is the place where the old-timers, the most gifted storytellers of Crisfield, like to gather to swap tall tales and humorous anecdotes, many of which feature the "chicken-neckers" (amateur crabbers) and the watermen of the Chesapeake Bay area.

The small community of Panacea, Florida, in the coastal panhandle area, has held its annual Wakulla Blue Crab Festival since 1965. Every year during the first weekend in May, thousands of crab lovers migrate from all parts of the Southeast to Panacea's balmy gulf shores to indulge in a variety of dishes featuring this delectable seafood. Although the festival was originally designed as a local event, since 1987 there has been a larger effort to show off the fishing industry. Festivities include a five-kilometer run, a beauty pageant, a blessing of the fleet, music, and crafts displays.

Without a doubt, the biggest attraction in the Panacea crab fest is the crab-picking contest. The pickers stand back

Louisiana Tiny Crab Balls

1 pound crabmeat
2 egg whites, lightly beaten
1/4 cup light sour cream
1/2 cup minced green onions
1 Tbls. fresh lemon juice
1 cup bread crumbs
1/2 tsp. dill weed

In a large bowl, blend the crabmeat, egg whites, sour cream, green onions, and lemon juice. Form into tiny, 1-inch diameter balls. Combine the bread crumbs and the dill. Roll the balls in the crumb mixture. Place crab balls on a large, greased or non-stick baking sheet and bake in a preheated oven at 375° for about 15 minutes. Serve with toothpicks as a party food.

Florida Crab Balls

6 ounces crabmeat
3 ounces untoasted bread crumbs
Salt and pepper to taste
2 eggs, beaten separately
1 tsp. fresh lemon juice
Toasted bread crumbs
Oil for deep-frying

Flake the crabmeat and mix with untoasted bread crumbs, salt, pepper, 1 of the eggs, and lemon juice. Divide into 8 to 12 portions and shape into balls. Use the other egg and the toasted breadcrumbs to coat each ball. Deep-fry in vegetable oil until golden brown. Drain well.

California Tortilla Crab Roll-Ups

1 8-ounce package cream cheese
8 ounces crabmeat
1 green onion, minced
10 stuffed olives, sliced
2 Tbls. seafood cocktail sauce
2 or 3 large flour tortillas

Mix together first five ingredients. Spread this concoction on the tortillas and roll them up. Refrigerate. Cut ½-inch slices and serve. (Note: these may be frozen in a large plastic bag and taken out just before serving at a party.)

Caribbean Crab Rangoon

1 8-ounce package cream cheese
2 tsp. minced fresh ginger
½ tsp. minced garlic
½ pound crabmeat
24 to 32 won ton pastry pieces
1 egg yolk, beaten well
Oil for deep-frying

Thoroughly blend cream cheese, ginger and garlic. Gently stir in crabmeat. Place heaping teaspoonful of crab mixture in center of each won ton pastry. Fold pastry over filling in any shape desired, making sure to seal the pastry tightly. Seal the pastry folds with beaten egg yolk. Fry in batches in hot oil until crisp and golden brown. Serve hot with dipping bowls of soy sauce and of sweet and sour sauce. (These sauces can be purchased at the grocery store and/or Chinese food stores.)

from the table as a pile of thirty or forty steamed crabs is dropped in front of each of them. Contestants have five minutes to pick claw and body meat. The winner, who must have the greatest weight with the least amount of cartilage or shell, gets $150 in prize money—not bad for five minutes of work.

The winners of the Panacea beauty festival used to be crowned the Blue Crab Queen. However, since the contestants didn't really like that title, a few years ago it was changed to Miss Wakulla. Although less descriptive than the former title, it sounds a lot better than Crisfield's Miss Crustacean.

The Crab Festival in LaCombe, Louisiana, is another annual summer event late in the month of June. LaCombe is a very small town located on the bayou of the same name that empties into Lake Pontchartrain on the north shore, across from New Orleans. It features soft-shell crab po-boy sandwiches made on crisp French bread, crab races, and lots of good family fun.

When the weather cools down in October, the little

fishing hamlet of Lafitte, Louisiana, south of New Orleans, has its St. Anthony church fair. The church is the hub of this small fishing and crabbing community. The fair features good food, music and dancing, crafts, games of chance, and crab races. No trophies are given to the winners. The object is to make gambling fun and at the same time to raise money for the church.

The crabs are outfitted with small tags bearing numbers. They are placed in separate starting boxes atop a large, painted plywood ramp that is kept wet during the races. Gamblers pick their favorite crabs and place bets at a dollar a ticket. At the start of the race, the boxes are opened simultaneously, and the crabs, with the help of gravity, scramble down to the finish line urged on by their sponsors. The winning crabs are not bedecked with flowers; instead, they wind up in the gumbo pot later in the day. Ah, what price, glory!

Indian Myths

In central India live a primitive group of blacksmiths

Chinese Crab Rangoon

A Chinese version of Crab Rangoon can be made with just the cream cheese and lump crabmeat, in equal portions, inside each won ton pastry. The finished rangoons are delicious just as they are—or even better served with a sweet sauce mixed with Chinese hot mustard for dipping.

Chinese Crabmeat Spring Rolls with Sauce

1 pound crabmeat
2 cups fresh bean sprouts
1 cup cooked rice noodles
1 bunch fresh cilantro, chopped
½ cup grated jicama root
½ cup blanched grated carrot
¼ cup grated cucumber
2 Tbls. chopped green onions
1 Tbls. rice vinegar
1 package won ton wrappers
Oil for deep-frying

Crab races, Lafitte, Louisiana. Photo by Frank Methe.

Mix ingredients together, except wrappers, and set aside. Peel off 1 sheet of won ton wrapper and dip in water to soften. Place about 2 tablespoons of filling on wrapper and roll the contents, folding in the sides as you go along. Use more water to seal the spring roll. Fry in batches in hot oil until crisp and golden brown. This recipe makes about 30 spring rolls which can be served immediately with dipping sauce or frozen in an air-tight plastic container and used later.

Sauce

½ cup seasoned rice vinegar
1 tsp. crushed red chillies
1 Tbls. chopped green onions
1 small piece ginger, crushed
1 clove garlic, crushed

Combine ingredients and mix well. Make the sauce a day ahead and store in the refrigerator.

Italian Crab and Spinach Raviolis

12 won ton wrappers
2 Tbls. butter
6 ounces crabmeat
4 ounces blanched spinach
½ green onion, chopped
1 sprig tarragon, chopped
Dash of Pernod (optional)
Salt and pepper to taste

Drop half of the won ton wrappers into a pot of boiling water and boil for 2 to 3 minutes. Let them cool in the water. Boil the other half of the wrappers, and let them cool. Melt the butter in a skillet and sauté the crabmeat and spinach with the green onions, tarragon, and Pernod. Simmer about 2 minutes until all the liquid has evaporated. Remove from the pan, and

known as the Agaria. In their principal creation myth, the Great Crab is called Kekramal Ch-hatri. He has the role of the Earth Diver.

First God made the world by laying a great lotus leaf on the face of the water. But the Sun arose and withered that leaf with his heat. Next, God made the world of lac. But when he climbed on it, it broke into a thousand pieces. So God made a crow from the dirt on his chest, and ordered the crow to fly in search of the earth. The crow grew weary of looking for the earth and dropped on top of the body of the Great Crab. The crab went down below the primordial waters and brought forth earth in little balls. The crow took the earth balls back to his father, and with them, God made the world.

When God finished creating the world, he went again to the crab and said, "Now the earth is ready, but there are no living creatures for it." So Kekramal Ch-hatri pulled five living creatures out of his side. The first was the Agaria people, and the others became all the tribes living in the world.

The Gond people, who intermarry with the Agaria, have the following myth about how the crab got its claws with the help of the blacksmiths.

In former times the crab had no claws. One day a Gond woman went to the river to fish. Under a large stone she found a crab and caught it. As she was about to kill it, the crab folded its hands and said, "Mother, don't kill me; keep me in your house and I will make all arrangements for you."

The woman took the crab home. A few days afterward the raja sent his servants to call the villagers to come to his fields to cut the crop. When they came to the woman's house, she had neither husband nor son to send to the fields. But the crab said, "Don't be afraid, Mother, I will go instead."

She went to the Agaria's smithy and got him to make two small knives of iron. She fixed the knives in front of the crab's body and by her magic ensured that it would be able to cut anything it desired.

The crab went to the raja's fields and cut a whole field by itself and piled up the grain. It returned to the woman's house and she was pleased and sent it back to live in the river.

season with salt and pepper. Allow the mixture to cool. Drain the boiled won tons and lay them on a clean, flat surface. Put a tablespoon of crab mixture in the middle of each and fold all the sides of the pastry into the middle to close tightly. Steam the raviolis on a rack over simmering water in a covered pan or wok for about 3 minutes.

Sauce
½ cup semi-dry white wine
1 green onion, chopped
1 cup chicken stock
¾ cup heavy cream
1 bunch fresh chives, chopped

Simmer the wine and green onion in a saucepan until it is reduced by half. Add the chicken stock and cream and continue reducing until a nice thickness is obtained. Add the chives at the last minute. Arrange the raviolis on a plate and cover with the sauce.

Polynesian Crab Dip

½ pound crabmeat
1 cup shredded coconut
2 cups sour cream
1 tsp. onion powder
2 tsp. curry powder
Salt and pepper to taste

Flake the crabmeat in a large bowl. Finely chop the shredded coconut and mix with the crabmeat. Add the rest of the ingredients. Chill for at least 1 hour. Serve with crackers or Melba toast.

Belgian Endive Stuffed with Crab Salad

Leaf lettuce
2 Belgian endives
½ pound crabmeat
⅓ cup crab cocktail sauce
Cherry tomatoes for garnish

Arrange the lettuce leaves on a serving platter and set aside. Trim ⅛-inch off the stem end of the endive and separate the leaves. Clean and wash them carefully. Dry them in a clean dish cloth or on paper towels. In a bowl, mix the crabmeat with the cocktail sauce. Stuff each endive leaf with a tablespoon of the crab mixture and arrange on the serving platter. Garnish with the cherry tomatoes. This dish can be fixed ahead of time and kept in the refrigerator for up to 2 hours before serving.

John Schluter's Mushrooms Stuffed with Crabmeat

1 pound fresh mushroom caps
¼ cup plus 3 Tbls. melted butter, separated
3 Tbls. bread crumbs
2 Tbls. minced celery
½ tsp. minced onion
¼ tsp. dry mustard
½ pound crabmeat
½ cup light sour cream
½ cup mayonnaise
3 Tbls. milk
2 tsp. lemon juice

Remove stems from mushrooms. Put mushrooms (round side up) on a baking sheet. Brush the tops with the ¼ cup

Tribal peoples from the Orissa region of central India have the following myth of how the crab came into being:

There was a potter, a mighty rogue. He purposely made his pots in such a way that they would break quickly and so force his customers to come and buy new ones. After a time his neighbors wearied of his tricks and gave him such a beating that he died. They carried his body to a stream and threw it in, saying: "Now make your pots in the water and try your tricks on the crocodiles and little fishes."

The potter's body turned into a crab. That is why the crab is always afraid of human beings and yet at the same time is very cunning.

melted butter and broil 4 inches from the heat for 3 minutes until lightly browned. In a large bowl, mix the bread crumbs, 3 tablespoons melted butter, celery, onion, and mustard. Stir in the crabmeat. Fill each mushroom cap with the crab mixture. In the flat pan of a chafing dish, combine the sour cream, mayonnaise, milk, and lemon juice. Cook and stir over hot water until hot. Arrange the filled mushrooms, rounded side down, in the sauce. Heat thoroughly. Serve immediately.

French Baked Stuffed Mushroom Caps

1½ cups lump crabmeat
4 Tbls. minced green onions
2 Tbls. butter
1 cup béchamel sauce
Salt and white pepper to taste
½ tsp. lemon juice
18–24 2-inch mushroom caps

Preheat the oven to 350°. Lightly shred the crabmeat. Sauté the green onion in butter; add crabmeat for 10 seconds and transfer to a large bowl. Stir in the béchamel sauce and season to taste with salt and pepper and lemon juice. Lightly grease a shallow baking dish or pan big enough to hold the mushroom caps in one layer. Sprinkle the inside of each cap with salt; spoon the crab mixture in each cap and arrange on the pan. Bake in the top of the oven 10 to 15 minutes or until the caps can be easily pierced with a fork and the filling is bubbly. Serve on a large heated platter.

Béchamel Sauce
6 Tbls. butter
3 cups milk, scalded (brought to a complete boil)
Salt to taste

Pinch of nutmeg
2 egg yolks, beaten well

Melt the butter in a saucepan; add the flour gradually, stirring constantly with a whisk, until it begins to turn a golden color. Slowly add hot milk, stirring constantly, so that the mixture does not become lumpy. Cook until mixture thickens and starts boiling. Remove from heat and stir in salt, nutmeg and egg yolks. Mix well. Return to moderate heat, stirring constantly until mixture is very creamy.

Southern Toasted Crab Canapés

3 Tbls. grated Parmesan cheese
1 cup mayonnaise
½ pound crabmeat
40 thin slices of onion
40 white bread triangles

Mix the cheese, mayonnaise, and crabmeat. Place a thin slice of onion on top of each piece of bread and top with the cheese mixture. Put on a non-stick baking sheet and sprinkle with extra grated Parmesan cheese. Place in the refrigerator for 2 hours. Broil until the tops are bubbly and brown.

Betty Gray's Crabbies

6 Tbls. softened butter
1½ tsp. mayonnaise
1½ 5-ounce jars Kraft Old English Cheese Spread, softened
½ tsp. salt
½ tsp. garlic salt
½ pound crabmeat
6 English muffins, split

Combine all ingredients except crabmeat and muffins, blending well with an electric mixer. Gently fold in the crabmeat so as not to break it up too much. Spread mixture onto muffin halves and place on baking sheet. Crabbies can be covered and refrigerated at this point to be broiled later. Or they can be frozen on the cookie sheet and then sealed in plastic bags for storage. Thaw before broiling. When ready to serve, broil in a preheated oven for 5 minutes until bubbly and slightly browned. Variation: Cut each muffin into bite-size pieces (6 to 8 pieces) to serve as small canapés.

Southern Crabmeat and Asparagus Canapés

6 English muffins
1 pound crabmeat
1 cup sliced almonds
½ cup minced celery
½ cup mayonnaise
2 Tbls. lemon juice
24 cooked asparagus spears
6 1-ounce slices Cheddar cheese
Paprika for garnish

Split the muffins in half; toast and butter them. In a bowl, combine the crabmeat, almonds, celery, mayonnaise, and lemon juice. Place the muffin halves on a cookie sheet. Place 2 asparagus spears on each muffin half. Cover each with about ⅓ cup of the crab mixture. Cut each cheese slice diagonally into quarters. Place two triangles on each muffin. Sprinkle with paprika and bake at 400° for 15 to 20 minutes or until heated thoroughly and cheese is melted. When cool, slice each muffin into quarters. (Note: the muffins also may be served whole as open-face sandwiches.)

West Coast Artichoke and Crab Cocktail

1 cup cooked artichoke hearts
1 cup crabmeat
½ cup cream
1 cup mayonnaise
½ cup catsup
½ tsp. Worcestershire sauce

Dice the artichoke hearts and mix with the crabmeat. Chill. Whip cream; add mayonnaise, catsup and Worcestershire sauce. Mix well, season to taste, and chill. Combine the two mixtures.

Crab Varieties

All crabs are not created equal—some have more meat and more flavor than others. The Calappas crab from the Mediterranean and warmer oceans (genus *Calappa*) is a delicacy in Spain and Italy. The German rock crab (*Cancer pagurus*) is a favorite item on European menus. Also in Europe, the edible crab (*Cancer pagurus*) is caught in large numbers in pots off the coasts. The total catch of the edible crab in 1973 was twenty-five million pounds.

On the Atlantic coasts of both North America, Central America, and South America, the blue crab (*Callinectes sapidus* Rathbun) is a most important source of food. It is so named because in Greek, *Callinectes* means beautiful swimmer, and this crab truly is a swimming beauty. *Sapidus* in Latin means tasty or savory. The last part of the name is a reference to the late Dr. Mary J. Rathbun of the Smithsonian Institution, who first gave the crab its specific name. Of the 998 new crab species that she identified and described, this

Salads & More

Crab Varieties

Chinese Myths

Crab Language

Aesop's Fables

Creole Stuffed Tomatoes

3 cups crabmeat
¹⁄₂ cup chopped celery
¹⁄₂ cup minced green onions
¹⁄₂ teaspoon dill weed
2 Tbls. olive oil
2 Tbls. lemon juice
4 medium tomatoes
Lettuce
2 hard-cooked eggs
Mayonnaise

Combine crabmeat, celery, onions, dill, oil, and lemon juice. Mix well. Refrigerate until ready to use. Slice the tops off the tomatoes. Scoop out the pulp and reserve for another use. Drain the tomatoes by turning them upside down on a paper towel. Arrange the lettuce on individual cold plates. Place a tomato shell on each plate and stuff with the crabmeat mixture. Garnish with hard-cooked egg wedges and serve with plain or caper-flavored mayonnaise.

SERVES 4

Creole Crab and Shrimp Salad

1 cup crabmeat
½ cup mayonnaise
½ tsp. Creole mustard
Dash Worcestershire sauce
¼ cup minced green onions
1 head of iceberg lettuce, washed and chopped fine
1 cup cooked, peeled shrimp
2 Tbls. catsup
Juice of ½ lemon
2 hard-cooked eggs, chopped
Tabasco sauce to taste
Tomato wedges or whole cherry tomatoes for garnish

Mix all ingredients together right before serving. Garnish with tomatoes.

SERVES 4

Creole Crabmeat Ravigote

Ravigote comes from the French word *ravigoter*, which means "to invigorate." The following recipe is composed of ingredients which are said to "revitalize the palate."

1 cup mayonnaise
1 Tbls. minced green pepper
1 Tbls. minced green onions

was the only one she labelled "savory." The reason for the name *sapidus* may be a matter of taste, and therefore outside the realm of scientific objectivity, but no crab in the world has been as much caught or as eagerly consumed as the *sapidus*.

Commercially speaking, the blue crab is the third most important crustacean, following shrimp and lobster, harvested in the United States. Among the edible crabs harvested and eaten in our country, it is the most popular. Blue crab production averages over fifty million pounds yearly. Although four native crabs are marketed heavily (blue crabs, Dungeness crabs, Alaska king crabs, and Florida stone crabs), many seafood fanciers think the meat of the blue crab is the best.

"Rock crab" is a common name for a number of crabs in the family Cancridae that includes the Jonah crab of the western Atlantic, the edible crab of Europe, and the Dungeness crab of the eastern Pacific.

The common rock crab (*Cancer irroratus*) is found offshore and in deep waters from New England to Florida and the Bahamas. The delicious and large Jonah crab (*Cancer borealis*) is only abundant in certain areas of the northeast, especially between Long Island and Nova Scotia.

The lady crabs, also called calico and sand crabs (*Ovalipes ocellatus ocellatus and Ovalipes o. guadulpensis*), are found between Nova Scotia and South Carolina. They like to nip the feet of bathers along Atlantic beaches. Since they are small (three inches across), they are eaten infrequently but the meat is of good flavor.

The stone crab, *Menippe mercenaria* of the Atlantic coast from North Carolina to Florida and *Menippi adina* of the Gulf Coast from Florida to Mexico, is a true gourmet food.

Stone crabs are, however, commercially landed only in Florida. They have very large claws that are quite valuable as well as tasty. Stone crabs (like all crabs) have the ability to cast off their legs or pincers if they are caught by one leg or experience extreme changes in temperature. The separation always occurs at one of the joints to protect the crab from bleeding. New appendages are grown in a process that takes about eigh-

1 Tbls. minced anchovies
1 Tbls. minced pimento
1 tsp. minced capers
1 pound lump crabmeat
1 head iceberg lettuce, shredded

Mix first six ingredients together and chill. Mix the sauce gently with crabmeat, being careful not to break up the meat. Chill in the refrigerator for one hour and serve on a bed of lettuce. Crabmeat ravigote also makes a delicious stuffing for ripe avocados.

SERVES 4

Southern Crab Salad Ravigote

3 cups crabmeat
1 Tbls. minced parsley
1/2 cup mayonnaise, divided
1 Tbls. fresh lemon juice
1 Tbls. chopped green onion
2 Tbls. sweet pickle relish
1 hard-cooked egg, chopped
Salt and pepper to taste
Salad greens
2 Tbls. chopped stuffed olives
1/2 tsp. paprika
Pimento strips

Mix first 8 ingredients (use half of the mayonnaise) and shape into a mound atop the salad greens. Mix the rest of the mayonnaise with the chopped olives and paprika, and spread this over the salad. Chill and garnish with pimento strips.

SERVES 4

Crab Louis Salad (for One)

Lettuce
Meat and legs of 1 Dungeness or king crab, or 1 cup crabmeat
Pimento
3 slices of tomato
1 hard-cooked egg, halved
Pickles and olives for garnish
1/2 green pepper, seeds removed

On a bed of lettuce, scatter the crabmeat and the cracked legs. Garnish with strips of pimento. On the side of the plate, arrange the tomato slices, egg halves, pickles, and olives. Put the Crab Louis sauce inside the green pepper half and place on the lettuce.

Sauce

1 cup crab cocktail sauce
1/4 cup chopped sweet pickle
2 Tbls. fresh lemon juice
1/4 cup chopped green pepper
2 Tbls. chopped onion

Mix the above ingredients and chill for at least 30 minutes.

West Coast Fruited Crab Compote

1 6–8 ounce package frozen Alaska king crabmeat
1 1/2 cup seedless green grapes
1/2 cantaloupe, cut into bite-sized chunks
1 8-ounce can pineapple chunks, drained
Sour cream dressing

Thaw, drain and slice crab. Layer fruits and crab in individual stemmed cocktail glasses. Serve with sour cream dressing.

teen months. Stone crabs are caught in traps; then, one large claw is popped off each, and they are returned to the sea to grow new nippers. This is truly ecological crab-harvesting.

The land crab (*Cardisoma guanhumi*), also called the white or mulatto crab, is found in Bermuda, from southern Florida and the Bahamas through the West Indies, and from Texas to Brazil. Although it lives on land, it reproduces in the sea. It reaches large size and the meat is sweet. It is an edible crab, but it is not harvested commercially.

Because land crabs feed mainly on carrion, many people will not eat them. However, a technique was developed (possibly by Native Americans) for the harvesting of these large crustaceans. In rural areas around Miami, such as the outskirts of Homestead, Florida, people would catch land crabs during their two annual migrations to the sea for reproduction. The crabs were then kept in wooden boxes for about a month and fed corn and other vegetable foodstuffs. They were then considered fit for consumption.

The golden crab (*Chaceon fenneri*) is Florida's newest crab fishery. It is harvested by wire traps set in deep waters offshore and is becoming increasingly popular with consumers domestically as well as abroad. This exotic new "discovery" is fast becoming a menu favorite in restaurants throughout southern Florida.

The red crab (*Cancer productus*) is caught with specialized trapping methods from the outer continental shelf off the East Coast. These large crabs have meat that is similar in flavor and appearance to the red king crab of the Pacific Ocean, although they have smaller legs and claws. They are becoming increasingly sought after, because of the great scarcity of red king crab from Alaska.

"Snow crab" is a market name for various crabs from around the world that have long legs and bodies covered with a dense growth of spines or chitinous hairs. The world's largest crab, the Japanese spider crab (*Macrocheir kaempferi*), as well as other large types, are marketed under the names snow crab, Tanner crab, and queen crab. The spinous spider

Sour Cream Dressing

1 cup dairy sour cream
2 Tbls. finely chopped chutney
1 Tbls. lime juice
½ tsp. curry powder

Mix the ingredients well. Cover; refrigerate several hours. Makes about 1 cup dressing. (Recipe courtesy Alaska Department of Fish and Game.)

Warm Crab Salad with Ginger Vinaigrette

½ cup flour
Salt to taste
Black pepper to taste
Lemon pepper to taste
Seasoned salt to taste
Juice of 3 limes
2 Tbls. chopped fresh cilantro
1½ inch fresh ginger, peeled
2 large garlic cloves, peeled
1 tsp. cayenne pepper
1 tsp. soy sauce
1 tsp. sesame oil
½ cup peanut oil, divided
¾ pound mozzarella cheese, cut into ½-inch cubes
1 pound Alaska king crab legs, peeled
1 bunch leaf lettuce, torn

Season the flour with salt, pepper, lemon pepper, and seasoned salt. Set aside. In blender or food processor, mix lime juice, cilantro, ginger, garlic, cayenne pepper, soy sauce, sesame oil and half of the peanut oil; blend until smooth. Place mozzarella cubes in a bowl; pour lime juice mixture over them and cover loosely. Set aside for ½ to 1 hour. Dredge crab legs in seasoned flour. Heat remaining peanut oil until *hot*. Fry crab legs about 2 minutes on each side until lightly browned and crispy. (Add more oil as needed.) Arrange lettuce on a large serving platter. With a slotted spoon, remove cheese from lime marinade and arrange in a circle on the lettuce. Place the hot fried crab legs in the center, and drizzle all with the marinade. Serve at once with a hot, crusty sourdough bread and fresh fruit.

SERVES 4

Aunt Vivian's Warm Crab and Fruit Salad

1 bunch leaf lettuce, torn in pieces
½ cantaloupe, cut in small pieces
1 peeled and diced orange
1 pear or apple, cored and thinly sliced
½ cup chopped pecans
½ pound Alaska king crab legs, cut into small pieces

Arrange the greens, fruit and pecans on 4 plates. Combine dressing ingredients; blend well. Add crab chunks to the dressing and cook over medium heat for 3 to 5 minutes, gently stirring until boiling. Remove crabmeat chunks and arrange atop each salad; top with warm dressing. Serve immediately.

SERVES 4

Dressing
½ cup orange juice
¼ cup light salad oil
1 Tbls. Dijon mustard
1 tsp. minced mint leaves

crab of Europe (*Maia squinado*) is very important in French cuisine, where it is called *araignée de mer*. Over thirty million pounds were harvested in Europe in 1973.

On the West Coast of the United States, the delicious Dungeness crab (*Cancer agister*) supports a large fishery from California to British Columbia, and in Alaska as well. The Dungeness crab is also known as the market crab and the common edible crab. Alaskans affectionately call it Dungee. It is the largest edible true crab on the West Coast. Much more information on this delicious crustacean is to be found on pages 94–111.

King or stone crabs are found around the world. Commercial fisheries exist in the Falkland Islands, Argentina, Chile, Peru, New Zealand, Australia, Japan, Russia, Alaska, and Canada. The Alaskan king crab is sometimes called the Japanese crab. Not a true crab, it is a relative of the hermit crabs. A deep-water type, it is yet another popular food source from our western waters.

In Alaska there are three different commercial king crab species: the red king crab (*Paralithodes camtschatica*), the blue king crab (*P. platypus*), and the golden king crab (*Lithodes aequispina*). These crabs have relatively small bodies with large, meaty legs and claws.

The oyster crab (*Pinnioteres pisun*) is the smallest of all edible crabs. Found in many parts of the world, the perpetually soft-shell females live inside oysters, clams, and mussels without harming their hosts. This arrangement is called commensalism. A few oyster-packing houses collect these very tasty, tiny crabs since there is a profitable market for them. The horse clam of the Pacific Ocean is large enough to support two or three little "pea crabs" of this type, making collecting easier for the fishermen.

Chinese Myths

According to Chinese mythology, in the old days all the animals could speak just the same as men. But they were always betraying the secrets of heaven, for which the deities punished them with dumbness. In those days the crab was still round and smooth.

Aunt Vivian's Avocado, Crab, and Citrus Salad

2 oranges
1 grapefruit
1 ripe avocado
½ pound cooked Alaska king crab legs, cut in chunks
2 Tbls. minced crystallized ginger
1 cup light sour cream
2 Tbls. mayonnaise
1 Tbls. honey
1 bunch leaf lettuce, arranged on 4 plates

Peel the oranges and grapefruit. Remove all membranes from the sections and cut in small chunks. Place in a large bowl. Peel and cut the avocado in small chunks and add to the fruit. Add the crabmeat and ginger. Toss lightly. Prepare the salad dressing by mixing the sour cream, mayonnaise, and honey together well. Pour over the salad and mix gently. Divide into 4 portions and place atop the salad greens.

SERVES 4

Crab Salad Ring

2 cups water
¼ cup minced green onions
2 cups fresh watercress leaves
½ cup minced parsley
2 tsp. dried tarragon, crumbled
4 tsp. plain gelatin
1½ cups mayonnaise
1½ pounds lump crabmeat
½ cup minced celery
Lettuce and cherry tomatoes for garnish

Bring 1½ cups of water to a boil. Add the green onions and cook for 2 minutes. Add the watercress, parsley, and tarragon, and boil for another minute. Discard the liquid, drain the greens and herbs thoroughly, and puree them in a food processor. Heat the remaining ½ cup water in the top of a double boiler; when it is warm, stir in the gelatin. Continue stirring until gelatin is completely dissolved.

Place the gelatin in a large bowl and allow to cool. Add the mayonnaise and puree. Fold in the crabmeat and celery, and pour into a one-quart ring mold. Smooth the top. Cover with foil or plastic wrap and refrigerate until the salad is firm to the touch. Unmold the ring by passing a knife around the edges and then setting the ring in a pan of hot water. Invert a chilled salad plate on top of the ring and turn over. Tap the plate on the table; the mold should slide out. Place lettuce leaves and cherry tomatoes around the salad ring and serve with crackers.

SERVES 4–6

Oregon Coast Crab Mold

1 envelope plain gelatin
4 Tbls. cold water
1 8-ounce package cream cheese
1 cup plus 3 Tbls. mayonnaise
1 can cream of mushroom soup
1 pound crabmeat
1 cup minced celery
3 green onions, thinly sliced
Crackers or wheat thins

Dissolve gelatin in cold water and set aside. Mix cream cheese and mayonnaise together. Over very low heat, stir and bring cheese mixture barely to a boil; take off heat. Add gelatin and stir well. Add mushroom soup, crab, celery, and onions. Blend well. Pour into a nonstick sprayed mold or small deep

One day a cow was secretly eating rice in a field when a red crab saw it and began to shout, "The cow is stealing rice! The cow is stealing rice!" The cow crossly told the crab to mind its business but the crab took no notice and merely shouted louder. This so enraged the cow that she lifted up her foot and stamped on it. The poor crab was squashed flat, and today one still sees the mark of a cow's hoof on the shells of crabs.

Crab Language
The dictionary's first definition of "crab" is a straightforward, unbiased one: "any of numerous chiefly marine broadly built crustaceans." Yet we often use the word in ways that could bruise the feelings of even the most hard-shelled crab.

In our everyday speech we use the word quite negatively. For example, ill-tempered people who are sullen or complain peevishly are called "crabs." "Crabby" people are no fun to be around since they are crosspatches gone sour on life. The word "crabbed" means "difficult to read or understand," as in crabbed handwriting. Crab apples are sour. Crab grass is a pest both in yards and in cultivated fields. And to add insult to injury, we have named the nasty lice that get in people's pants crabs! Consider, for example, the following bit of latrinalia collected from a so-called "ladies'" room. "No need to stand upon the seat, the crabs in here can jump six feet!"

To be sure, we sometimes use the word just as a descriptive term, without the negative associations. But only two examples come to mind, and they are somewhat obscure. First, there is the Crab Nebula, discovered in A.D. 1054 by the Chinese but so named by Europeans in 1850 because of its shape. But how many of us have seen, or even heard of, the Crab Nebula? Then there is the Christmas or crab cactus that blooms in December and gets its name because its dark green branches resemble crab legs.

Why do we heap such verbal abuse upon crabs? Is it because some crabs are carnivorous scavengers? The same is true for lobsters, but they don't receive such treatment.

bowl. Chill overnight. Before serving, unmold onto a plate and surround with assorted crackers. (See Crab Salad Ring, p. 45, for directions in unmolding.) Provide a butter knife for spreading. (Note: imitation crab or lobster may be substituted.)
SERVES 4–6

Mexican Avocado and Crabmeat Mousse

1 Tbls. dry sherry
1 Tbls. fresh lime juice
1 chicken stock cube
1 envelope plain gelatin
1 Tbls. water
1 large, ripe avocado, peeled and chopped
2 Tbls. heavy cream
3–4 drops Tabasco sauce
2 Tbls. mayonnaise
½ tsp. ground cumin
½ pound lump crabmeat
Salt and white pepper to taste
Lettuce
Tomato wedges for garnish
Crackers or toast points

Combine sherry, lime juice, chicken stock cube, gelatin, and water in small saucepan. Allow gelatin to soften (about 5 minutes). Heat mixture to dissolve gelatin and stock cube. In a blender, combine avocado, cream, gelatin mixture, Tabasco, mayonnaise, and cumin. Blend until smooth; pour into large bowl. Gently fold in crabmeat. Add salt and pepper to taste. Pour mixture into a 1-quart mold and chill until set, 2 to 3 hours. To serve, unmold the avocado mousse onto a serving platter lined with lettuce leaves. Garnish with tomato wedges. Serve with crackers or toast points. (See recipe for Crab Salad Ring, p. 45, for directions in unmolding.)
SERVES 4

New Orleans Crab Salad

3 cups crabmeat
1/4 cucumber, peeled and chopped
1/4 cup chopped green pepper
1 cup cooked, chopped green beans
2 hard-cooked eggs, chopped
1/4 cup chopped raw cauliflower
1/2 cup minced celery
1 tsp. salt
1/4 tsp. pepper
1 large can artichoke hearts, drained and quartered
3/4 cup Thousand Island dressing
6 large tomato slices
6 lettuce leaves
Radish slices

Combine all ingredients except tomato, lettuce, and radishes. Toss lightly. Arrange 1 tomato slice on each lettuce leaf and place 1 cup of the salad on each. Garnish with the radish slices.

SERVES 6

Creole Crab Rémoulade

1 1/2 pounds lump crabmeat
1 head of iceberg lettuce, chopped in long, thin strips

Rémoulade Sauce
1/4 cup Zatarain's Creole mustard
1 Tbls. paprika
1 tsp. cayenne pepper
5 tsp. salt
1/2 cup tarragon vinegar
1 1/3 cups olive oil

Crabs are suspect in part because of the peculiar way in which they move around on land. They are swift and unpredictable runners. Without turning around, they can change directions, back up, or move sideways to the right or to the left. That makes them very hard to catch. We humans want more predictability in the animals we hunt for food, and crabs just won't oblige.

Besides their capacity for fancy footwork, crabs have another feature that makes us uneasy. They have better vision than we do; in fact, it is twice as good! Their compound eyes allow them not only to see form and color, but also to have a visual field of 360 degrees. Crabs have no blind spots as we do—they can see all around.

In addition, crabs have acute hearing abilities. With little hairs inside their leg joints, they are able to pick up even tiny vibrations made by anything coming in their direction on the beach or the ground.

Such good hearing and vision makes crabs highly conscious of their surroundings. As a result, they have very large flight distances. For example, the European fiddler crab can spot a tall man when he is nineteen meters away, even before the man's footsteps are felt in the sand. That gives the crab lots of time to run for cover, which probably means no crab for the hungry man's soup.

A sinister association occurred in ancient times, when in classic Greek the single word *karkinos* was used both for the crab and for the dreaded disease cancer. Not so in today's popular Greek, in which the feisty crab is called *kavóuri* (singular) or *kavóuria* (plural), but the disease is still called *karkinos*.

What caused the ancient Greeks to associate this particular animal with tumorous malignancies? Apparently, it had to do with the Mediterranean shore crab's behavior on the beach. The Potomon crabs move and spread out quickly and unpredictably on the sandy beach, just as cancer spreads quickly and unpredictably in the human body. This perceived similarity of movement was the basis, then, for the unfortunate association.

For the ancient Greeks, then, there was something sin-

1½ cups chopped green onions
½ cup minced celery
½ cup chopped parsley
Crackers or French bread

To make rémoulade sauce, combine Zatarain's Creole mustard, paprika, cayenne pepper and salt in a deep bowl and stir with a wire whisk until completely mixed. Beat in the vinegar. Beating constantly, pour in the oil slowly, in a thin stream, and beat until the sauce is smooth and thick. Add the green onions, celery, and parsley; mix well. Cover the bowl tightly and let sit at room temperature for at least 3 hours until serving.

Just before serving, arrange the shredded lettuce on top of chilled salad plates and arrange the lump crabmeat on the top. Spoon the rémoulade sauce over the crabmeat and serve at once, with crackers or French bread slices.

SERVES 4

Creole Surimi Crab Salad

1 8-ounce package surimi (imitation crabmeat), chopped
1 small can green beans, chopped
½ cup mayonnaise
1 green onion, chopped
2 medium celery stalks, chopped
3 Tbls. sweet pickle relish
1 Tbls. Zatarain's Creole mustard
3 drops Tabasco sauce
3 hard-cooked eggs, chopped
2 large tomatoes
Several leaves of iceberg lettuce, whole

Combine all ingredients except the lettuce and tomatoes. Cover and chill at least 1 hour before serving. Serve on a bed of lettuce with tomato wedges and crackers.

SERVES 2–4

Florida Colorful Crabmeat Salad

6 cups cooked sea shell pasta
1 pound crabmeat
1 cup cooked frozen green peas
½ cup diced red bell peppers
½ cup chopped red onions
½ cup chopped parsley
½ cup extra virgin olive oil
2 Tbls. fresh lemon juice
1 Tbls. basil
½ tsp. salt
½ tsp. minced garlic
¼ tsp. white pepper

Use colorful pasta such as beet, spinach, tomato, and egg. Combine the cooked pasta, crabmeat, peas, peppers, onions, and parsley in a large salad bowl; toss. Cover and refrigerate for 3 to 4 hours. Combine the oil, lemon juice, basil, salt, garlic and pepper in a jar with a tight-fitting cover and shake well. Pour salad dressing over salad just before serving. (Recipe courtesy Florida Department of Agriculture and Consumer Services, Bureau of Seafood and Aquaculture.)

SERVES 8

Artichokes Stuffed with Crab Dip

½ pound crabmeat
1 cup sour cream
1 8-ounce package cream cheese, softened
5 Tbls. fresh lemon juice
4 drops Tabasco sauce
1 tsp. seasoned salt
2 tsp. chopped chives
4 fresh, large artichokes
3 black peppercorns

ister about crabs. Over the centuries, their negative attitude has been passed down to us in Western Civilization, and survives today in the language we use.

In other words, if somebody calls you a crab, blame it on the Greeks. As for the crabs, let them get an attorney!

Aesop's Fables

In the western tradition, lessons and wisdom from the ages are contained in very short stories attributed to Aesop, a legendary Greek fabulist. Scholars continue to debate whether or not there really was a person named Aesop. Regardless of that issue, the stories known as Aesop's Fables continue to this day to provide bits of ancient truths. At least two fables feature crabs.

The Crab and Her Mother

Said an old crab to a young one, "Why do you walk so crooked, child?" "Mother," said the young crab, "show me the way, will you? And when I see you taking a straight course, I will try and follow."

Said Aesop: "Example is better than precept." Parents should set good examples for their children rather than "Do as I say, not as I do."

The Crab and the Fox

A crab, forsaking the seashore, chose a neighboring green meadow as its feeding ground. A fox came across him, and being very much famished, ate him up. Just as he was on the point of being eaten, the crab said, "I well deserve my fate; for what business had I on the land when by my nature and habits I am only adapted for the sea?"

Aesop said: "Contentment with our lot is an element of happiness." This fable suggests that when one is adapted to a particular place it is quite foolish to move to another.

To make the crab dip, flake the crabmeat. Blend sour cream and cream cheese; add the crab, 2 tablespoons of the lemon juice, Tabasco, salt, and chives. Cover and chill overnight to blend the flavors. To prepare the artichokes, remove the stem and tough outer leaves. Using scissors, cut the top from each artichoke and then cut off the prickly end of each petal. Rinse and place in boiling salted water containing 3 tablespoons lemon juice and 3 black peppercorns. Cover and cook for 30 minutes or until tender. Turn upside down to drain and cool. Pull out the center petals and remove the inedible part using a teaspoon to scrape the top of the artichoke heart. Fill the centers of the artichoke with the crab dip and use the leaves for dipping.

SERVES 4

Soups and Chowders & More

The Heavenly Crab

Crabs in New World Archaeology

Japanese Folktales

Creole Crab, Shrimp, and Okra Gumbo

Creole gumbo is probably the most famous of all Louisiana soup dishes. There are many ways to cook it and many varieties. Some include meats, such as sausage or fowl, and some feature seafood.

Crab, shrimp, and okra gumbo is truly a multicultural soup: Louisiana seafood thickened with an African vegetable, okra (or a native American herb, ground sassafras, called filé powder) and made with brown roux, a French soup, sauce, and gravy base.

The New Orleans-born anthropologist Stephen Duplantier once observed that Louisiana okra seafood gumbo, served over a scoop of boiled, white rice, is a visual metaphor for the murky swamps of our state, where floating islands of vegetation conceal an abundance of aquatic delicacies.

The Heavenly Crab

Mystery and romance have always been associated with the zodiac, that imaginary girdle encircling the earth through which the sun, moon, and planets pass during the year. The word "zodiac" is derived from Greek and means "little animals." The ancient Sumerian and Akkadian races who lived near the Euphrates River were the first to divide the zodiac into signs and symbols. Originally there were only six signs, and among the six was Cancer, the great heavenly crab.

In Greek mythology, the crab was one of the four fierce beasts of prey that Phaëthon, mortal son of the sun god Helios, had to elude the day he tried to drive his father's chariot up across the heavens. Phaëthon managed to steer the mighty horses past the bull, the lion, and the scorpion. But a near collision with the ferocious crab frightened him so badly he dropped the reins of the chariot. The horses ran wild and the chariot left the path, spreading fire and destruction all over the earth. To save mankind from certain destruction,

Jove hurled a thunderbolt at the rash young driver, killing him but sending the chariot safely back down into the sea. (The moral of the story is to watch out for big crabs on the highway when you borrow your father's car.)

Because Cancer was considered the most inconspicuous star figure in the zodiac, an apology for its being there was offered with another story in Greek mythology, which tells that when the crab was crushed by Hercules for pinching his toes during a fight with the Hydra in the marsh of Lerna, Juno took pity on the poor, squashed creature and exalted it to the sky.

Other early peoples thought the heavenly crab was connected with birth. The two bright stars in Cancer were, according to Chaldean and Platonist philosophy, the so-called Gate of Men through which souls descended from heaven into human bodies.

In contemporary astrology, those born between June 22 and July 21 bear the sign of the crab, the fourth sign of the zodiac. In spite of its name, Cancer is a homey, motherly sign,

1 pound raw, peeled shrimp
7 quarts water
1 tsp. Tabasco sauce
1 lemon, sliced
3 fresh bay leaves
1½ tsp. dried thyme, divided
1 Tbls. plus 1 tsp. salt, divided
12 live blue crabs
2 Tbls. vegetable oil
2 Tbls. flour
1 large onion, chopped
¾ cup minced celery
3 cloves garlic, minced
½ pound fresh okra, sliced
¾ cup chopped green pepper
1 tsp. cayenne pepper
6 cups cooked white rice

Devein the shrimp. Wash and set aside. In a 12-quart heavy soup pot, bring the water, Tabasco, sliced lemon, 2 bay leaves, 1 teaspoon thyme and 1 tablespoon of the salt to a boil. Drop in the live crabs and boil for 5 minutes. Remove with tongs and set aside to cool. Place the shrimp in the stock and cook for 3 minutes until they are firm. Remove with tongs. Continue to boil the stock until it has reduced to only about 3 quarts. Strain the stock and keep warm in a covered pot until ready to use.

Clean the crabs and pick out the meat, eggs, and fat. Save the claws. In a heavy 6-quart pot, make a roux by heating the oil and gradually adding the flour, stirring constantly until a very dark brown color is obtained. (The secret of a good gumbo is to cook the roux almost to the burning point. Have patience; this takes at least 10 to 15 minutes.) Remove from the fire and add the onions, celery, and garlic. Return to a low fire and stir constantly for about 5 minutes. Add the okra and green peppers and mix well. Add the warm stock little at a time, stirring constantly, and bring to a boil. Add the cayenne pepper, remaining bay leaf, ½ teaspoon of thyme and about 1 teaspoon salt. Stir in the crabmeat and the claws, reduce the heat to a simmer, and cook partially covered for 1 hour, stirring occasionally. Just before serving, add the shrimp and simmer two minutes longer. Taste to see if more Tabasco or salt is needed.

Each soup bowl should be prepared with a large scoop of cooked white rice, over which the gumbo is ladled. Have a jar of filé powder on the table for those who wish to add some

and also perhaps the most vulnerable. It is the sign of the summer solstice, from which time it will be nine months before Aries (a sign associated with male virility) comes around again. Hence it is a symbol of fertility and conception. Along with Pisces and Scorpio, it is a water sign. Because it is the first of the watery signs, it symbolizes the primeval waters and represents our origins.

Cancer is the northern zodiacal constellation between Gemini, the twins, and Leo, the lion. Today it is one of eighty-eight arbitrary configurations of stars seen in the celestial sphere.

People born under the sign of Cancer are supposed to have certain characteristics. Crabs, though soft inside, have hard shells and are difficult to dislodge from their chosen crannies. So throughout the centuries this sign has stood for tenacity. Motherly people and mother-fixated people are also associated with this sign. Being extremely sensitive, it is a sign of many colors and moods, although its official colors are russet and green. Many astrologers consider those born under

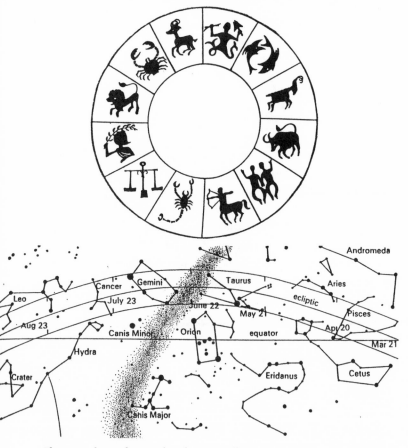

This map shows the actual Zodiac constellations in relation to the imaginary Zodiac band.

this sign to make excellent teachers, actors and actresses.

The zodiacal opposite to Cancer is Capricorn, an earthy no-nonsense sign that does not suffer from hypersensitivity. The signs that are congenial with Cancer are Pisces and Taurus.

In astrology, Cancer is the only sign ruled by the moon. The astrological spheres of influence of the moon are the feminine principle (fecundity, motherhood, the family), the soul, adaptation, the nation, and hereditary qualities.

This connection between the moon and the crab might explain why even the most pleasant-mannered person often feels "crabby" on moondays (Mondays)!

just before eating. (Note: never put the filé powder into the cooked okra gumbo in the pot, and cook or heat it, or the gumbo will become stringy.) Place a nutcracker on the table for opening the crab claws. Serve with hot French bread.

SERVES 12

Aunt Emma's Gulf Coast Gumbo

½ pound raw ham
½ pound raw veal
½ pound raw pork sausage
4 Tbls. vegetable oil
3 medium onions, chopped
½ pound fresh okra
1 large green pepper, chopped
Few parsley sprigs, minced
3 quarts boiling water
2 large cans tomatoes
Pinch of thyme
1 clove garlic, minced
2 fresh bay leaves, minced
Salt and pepper to taste
1 pound raw shrimp, peeled
1 pound blue crab claw meat

Cut ham, veal, and sausage into small pieces; sauté in oil together with the onion, green pepper, and parsley until browned. Add boiling water, tomatoes, okra, thyme, garlic, bay leaves, salt and pepper. Simmer at least 60 minutes, stirring occasionally. Add crabmeat and cook 30 minutes longer, stirring now and then. Five minutes before serving, add the shrimp and stir occasionally. Serve with steamed white rice, filé powder, and hot garlic French bread. (Gumbo is better made the day before and reheated after the flavors have mixed.)

SERVES 12 or more

Louisiana Easy Creole Crab Gumbo

½ cup chopped onion
4 Tbls. butter
4 Tbls. flour
1 pound okra, cleaned and sliced
1 cup chopped green pepper
2 crushed garlic cloves
5 cups canned tomatoes
1 pound crabmeat
1 tsp. ground nutmeg
1 whole bay leaf
Salt and pepper to taste
2 cups water

Chop the tomatoes or puree in a food blender. Sauté onion in the butter until translucent. Stir in the flour and brown. Slowly add the remaining ingredients, stirring constantly. Bring to a boil, reduce the heat, cover, and simmer for 1 hour stirring occasionally.

SERVES 8

Florida Blue Crab Gumbo

½ cup chopped onion
½ cup chopped celery
1 clove garlic, minced
¼ cup melted butter or oil
¼ tsp. crushed thyme
¼ tsp. sugar
1 whole bay leaf
½ tsp. pepper
Salt to taste
1 package frozen, sliced okra
2 20-ounce cans tomatoes

Crabs in New World Archaeology

The splendid archaic civilizations of the Pacific Coast regions of South America, which reached their peak with the Inca Empire by A. D. 1500, had deep roots in earlier cultures. As early as 3500 B. C. there were countless fishing villages flourishing along the rugged coast. Crabs were one of the more significant maritime edibles harvested in those prehistoric times.

More than just food, however, crabs held a special significance for the prehistoric Chavín peoples. At 2000 B. C. they produced remarkable cotton textiles bearing symmetrical, angular decorative motifs that included familiar designs from popular iconography. One such formalized art motif was the crab. The brightly colored cotton textiles re-created familiar myths and spirit creatures that inhabited the Chavín cosmos.

Around the time of the birth of Christ, the Chavín people were followed by the Moche, lords of Peru's north coast. Moche pottery is considered by archaeologists to be America's finest, the equivalent of the great classical Greek vases. Working without the potter's wheel, they mass-produced bowls, pots, and bottles painted with red, white, and earth-colored designs. The potters painted anthropomorphic owls, plants, serpents, warriors, musicians, moon gods, and humans making love with deities. They depicted events in the Moche creation stories and portrayed gods in their roles as crabs and other animals.

Recent archaeological work at two royal Moche tombs of the lords of Sipán disclosed priceless gold treasure. Walter Alva and other archaeologists discovered these riches hidden inside a huge pyramid. Among

1 pound crabmeat
3 cups cooked white rice

Sauté onion, celery, and garlic in oil or butter until tender. Add seasonings, okra, and tomatoes. Cover and simmer for 45 minutes, stirring occasionally. Remove bay leaf; add crabmeat. Serve over rice. (Recipe courtesy of the Florida Department of Agriculture and Consumer Services, Bureau of Seafood and Aquaculture.)
SERVES 6

Florida Blue Crab and Vegetable Gumbo

1 can chicken gumbo soup
2 soup cans water
1 package frozen, mixed vegetables
4 slices bacon, cooked and crumbled
3 Tbls. catsup
1 tsp. Old Bay powder
1 pound crabmeat

Place soup and water in a 3-quart saucepan. Cover and bring to a boil. Add frozen vegetables. Cover and bring to boil again. Reduce heat and cook 9 to 12 minutes or until vegetables are tender. Add bacon, catsup, Old Bay powder and crabmeat. Heat. Serve with hot French bread. (Recipe courtesy of the Florida Department of Agriculture and Consumer Services, Bureau of Seafood and Aquaculture.)
SERVES 4

Maryland Blue Crab Soup

2 Tbls. cooking oil
1 large onion, chopped

1 stalk celery, chopped
2 cloves garlic, crushed
1 large can tomato sauce
2 quarts stock from boiled crabs*
1 bay leaf
6 large blue crabs, boiled and cleaned (save the claws)
½ cup corn, cooked
½ cup green peas, cooked
½ cup green beans, cooked
Salt and pepper to taste
6 drops Tabasco

Sauté the onion, celery, and garlic in the cooking oil until tender. Add the tomato sauce, stock, and bay leaf; bring to a boil, reduce heat, and simmer for 30 minutes. Add the crabmeat and the rest of the ingredients, including the cracked crab claws, and bring to a boil again. Reduce the heat and simmer for 15 minutes. Serve with hot bread.

*You may substitute a good fish or shrimp stock if you desire.

SERVES 6 or more

Creole Creamy Crab Soup

1 cup boiling water
1 chicken bouillon cube
¼ cup butter
⅛ cup minced celery
¼ cup minced onion
3 tablespoons flour
1 teaspoon minced parsley
Salt and white pepper to taste
1 quart milk (at room temperature)
1 pound crabmeat
Dash of nutmeg (optional)

the priceless pieces were gold ornaments showing anthropomorphic figures of a crab and a feline. According to conventional interpretation, these figures combining animal and human features represented the hallucinogenic visions of shamans. The religion and cosmology of the Moche were rooted in ancient Andean beliefs, which were elaborated by Chavín shamans and their contemporaries and then refined by the coastal peoples to reflect the harsh challenges of a life constantly threatened by floods and the vagaries of the Pacific Ocean.

Moche culture went into a decline around A.D. 800. At that time, the Moche were being replaced in the north by the Chimú people, whose coastal culture flourished between A.D. 1000 and 1370. The pantheon of the Chimú included a crab god. He was the focus of a little-known religious cult in what is today northern Peru.

Both the crab and the crab god were depicted in a wide variety of ways in Chimú artwork. Most examples come from their pottery, where some crab designs were painted and others were modelled in relief. The Chimú also made crab figurines in clay, some of which were whistles. The crab god was embossed on metal, as well as being cut out of metal sheets, including gold. He was also included in woven designs in wool. Exquisite miniature gold figurines were made to represent this toothsome aquatic deity.

The crab divinity, most popular in early and middle Chimú times, sank into oblivion well before the Spanish conquest. For that reason there is no written information from the early Spanish chronicles about the cult.

Archaeologists presume, however, that the crab cult spread by boat northward to the west coast of the isthmus region of Central America. (The boat hypothesis results from a lack of prehistoric findings pertaining to the crab cult in Ecuador.) The same crab god is seen in pre-Columbian art and artifacts from Panama, Costa Rica, and even Nicaragua.

Because he was depicted quite realistically in early Chimú times, some of the crab

Dissolve the bouillon cube in the boiling water and set aside. Sauté the onion and celery in butter until transparent. Blend in the flour and add the seasonings. Add the milk and bouillon gradually and cook until thick, stirring constantly with a wire whisk. Add the crabmeat and cook another minute or two. Sprinkle top with nutmeg and parsley.

SERVES 6 or more

Louisiana Creole Crab Soup

1 stick butter
1 large onion, chopped
1 stalk celery, minced
2 cloves garlic, minced
1 Tbls. cornstarch
1 pound lump crabmeat
Salt to taste
Tabasco sauce to taste
1 quart scalded milk
2 Tbls. dry sherry
¼ cup chopped green onion tops

Melt butter and add all the vegetables except the green onion tops. Sauté until transparent, about 5 minutes. Add the cornstarch and mix well. Add the crabmeat, seasoned with salt and Tabasco sauce, and cook for 3 minutes. Slowly add scalded milk and stir until mixture thickens. Stir and simmer for 10 minutes. When finished, remove from the fire, add the sherry and stir well. Sprinkle with green onion tops.

SERVES 6 or more

West Coast Crab and Fish Chowder

1 pound fish
2 Tbls. margarine

8 Tbls. minced onion
1 cup chopped carrot
8 Tbls. minced celery
1/3 cup flour
Salt to taste
Dash of paprika
2 10-ounce cans chicken broth
3 cups skim milk
1 cup grated Cheddar and/or Monterey Jack cheese
1 pound crabmeat

Cut fish into 1-inch pieces. Melt margarine in saucepan and add onion, carrot, and celery. Cook until onion is transparent. Blend in flour, salt, and paprika to taste. Cook 1 minute, stirring constantly. Gradually add chicken broth and milk. Cook, stirring constantly, until thick. Add fish; simmer until fish flakes. Add cheese; stir until melted. Add crabmeat and cook a few minutes more to heat through.

SERVES 12

Louisiana Crab Bisque

1/4 cup butter or margarine
2 Tbls. minced onion
2 Tbls. minced celery
3 Tbls. flour
1/4 tsp. paprika
1 tsp. salt
1/8 tsp. white pepper
1 quart milk
1 pound crabmeat
Fresh parsley, chopped

In a large pot, melt the butter or margarine and sauté the onion and celery until transparent. Blend in the flour and sea-

god's attributes are apparent. He was evidently quite fierce, since his face appears contorted with rage. In addition to his crab legs, he was frequently given human legs and arms. There was a tendency to place his face on the back of his shell, a concept based perhaps on some long-forgotten religious symbolism. Most curious of all was the depiction of his tail, which was always shown in an unnaturally extended position.

Chimú crab god

In real life, crabs clamp their tails under their bodies. The projecting tail of the crab god, phallic-like in its appearance, gave him an air of extra virility. This suggests that he was the focus of a fertility cult. Certainly the male fiddler crabs from this region are blatantly amorous, a trait that has been noted time and again by naturalists such as William Beebe. The crab god was shown to have two enemies: a fish god whom he catches on a fish line, and a human-looking demon with large canine teeth who fights him with a hand axe.

Some of the finest examples of crab god art were produced by the Coclé people who lived in the central Pacific region of Panama and whose culture flourished between A.D. 500 and 1000. The site known as Sitio Conte has yielded numerous examples of fine polychrome pottery featuring stylized crabs, one of the most important motifs in all their artwork. Typical designs show boldly rendered crab patterns repeated four times on a circular design that has been divided into quarters. Crab bodies are often shown in a triangular form with elongated shoulders,

sonings. Add the milk gradually, stirring constantly. Cook until thick. Add the crabmeat and heat. Just before serving, sprinkle with parsley.

SERVES 6

Gulf Coast Quick Crabmeat Bisque

1 can cream of mushroom soup
1 can cream of asparagus soup
1½ soup cans milk
1 cup light cream
½ pound crabmeat
¼ cup dry sherry
Butter
Fresh parsley, chopped

In a saucepan, combine soups; stir in milk and cream. Heat to boiling over medium heat. Reduce heat. Add crabmeat; heat thoroughly, 3 to 4 minutes. Add sherry just before serving. Float a chunk of butter on top, and sprinkle with parsley.

SERVES 6

South Carolina She-Crab Soup

Just as seafood and okra gumbo is associated with New Orleans, she-crab soup is a well-loved and widely known specialty from Charleston, South Carolina. So popular is this delicacy that a poem was created to honor it:

> *She-Crab Soup*
> A soup to remember!
> The feminine gender
> of crabs is expedient—

the secret ingredient.
The flavor essential
makes men reverential
who taste this collation
and cry acclamation.

Anonymous

3 Tbls. minced celery
5 Tbls. minced red onion
$^1/_3$ cup plus 2 Tbls. light vegetable oil
$^1/_3$ cup flour, sifted
2 cups light cream
1 gallon milk
$1^1/_2$ cups dry sherry
1 pound lump crabmeat
$3^1/_2$ ounces fresh crab eggs* (or 8 hard-cooked eggs, chopped)
3–4 drops Tabasco
White pepper to taste
3 ounces chicken stock

Sauté celery and onion in 2 tablespoons oil until transparent. Set aside. In a different skillet, preferably an iron one, heat the remaining oil and gradually add the flour, stirring constantly, until a golden-colored roux is formed. Warm the cream and the milk in the top of a large double boiler, then add the cooked vegetables and the sherry. Heat the crabmeat in the skillet used for the onions and celery, then add to the milk mixture with the crab eggs. Season to taste with the Tabasco and white pepper, then add the chicken soup and the roux. Cook very slowly for 35 minutes. The soup may be made a day in advance. Many think it tastes better after setting for 24 hours in the refrigerator.

*Harris's Canned Crab Roe, packed in South Carolina, can be substituted for fresh crab eggs.

SERVES 12

five pairs of legs, and the unnaturally extended tail.

Japanese Folktales

The following story was collected in Kikai Island, Oshima-gun, Kagoshima-ken. Related versions are found all over Europe and in Africa, as well as in African American and Native American traditions. Aesop's fable "The Hare and the Tortoise" is a parallel story.

The Cat and the Crab

One day the cat and the crab decided to have a race. The cat thought, "No matter how fast the crab runs sideways, he will be no match for me," and so he took it easy. But just as they began the race, the sly crab attached himself to the cat's tail. The cat never noticed, starting as fast as he could run and soon coming to the goal. Wondering how the crab was doing, the cat turned around to take a look. At that very moment, the crab let loose his tail and called out, "Mr. Cat, are you just now arriving?"

The cat turned around in surprise, and sure enough, there was the crab with one foot over the goal line. The cat was beaten. Hanging his head, he admitted his defeat.

The next story also has a parallel in European folktales such as "The Cock, Hen, Duck, Pin, and Needle on a Journey," in which various strategically placed objects punish the evil one.

The Monkey and the Crab

Once upon a time, there lived a monkey and a crab. The monkey had a persimmon seed, and the crab had a pressed rice ball. The monkey said, "Mr. Crab, how about trading my persimmon seed for your rice ball?" So they traded.

The crab took the persimmon seed and planted it in his front field. Day by day it grew bigger and bigger, and after a while there were splendid persimmons on it. The crab went over to the monkey's place and asked him to come pick the persimmons for him. The monkey readily agreed and climbed up in the tree. But then he ate the ripe fruit himself and threw the green ones down at the poor crab!

The crab became angry and ran home, all the while calling the monkey bad names. This made the monkey furious, and he chased the crab into its hole. Then the monkey started to defecate into the crab's den.

So, the crab took his scissor claws and fastened them securely

Georgia She-Crab Soup

1 Tbls. butter
1 Tbls. flour
1 quart milk
2 cups crabmeat and eggs
3 drops onion juice
⅛ tsp. mace
Tabasco sauce to taste
½ tsp. Worcestershire sauce
Salt and white pepper to taste
Dry sherry, warmed
¼ pint cream, whipped
Minced parsley for garnish

Melt the butter in the top of a double boiler and blend with the flour until smooth. Add milk gradually, stirring constantly. Add crabmeat with eggs and all the seasonings, except the sherry. Cook slowly over the hot water for 20 minutes. To serve, place a tablespoon of warmed sherry in each soup bowl, then add the soup and top with whipped cream. Sprinkle with parsley. If she-crabs are not available, chop the yolks of hard-boiled eggs into the bowls before the soup is added.

SERVES 6

Georgia She-Crab Soup with Mushrooms

½ onion, grated
2 small celery stalks, minced
½ cup chopped fresh mushrooms
1 green onion, minced
2 Tbls. butter, divided
2 Tbls. flour
3 cups scalded milk
2 cups crabmeat with eggs

1 cup heavy cream
3 Tbls. dry sherry
1 Tbls. fresh lemon juice
1/8 tsp. grated lemon rind
1 Tbls. Worcestershire sauce
1/8 tsp. white pepper
1/8 tsp. mace
Salt and Tabasco sauce to taste

Sauté onion, celery, mushrooms, and green onion in 1 tablespoon butter. In the top of a double boiler, blend remaining butter and flour. Add the milk slowly, stirring until liquid is smooth and thickened. Add mushroom mixture and remaining ingredients. (If crab eggs are unavailable, substitute 2 chopped, hard-cooked eggs). Cook for 30 minutes over medium heat. DO NOT BOIL.

SERVES 6

Southern Crab and Corn Bisque

1/2 cup chopped celery
1/2 cup chopped green onions
1/4 cup chopped green pepper
1/2 cup melted butter
2 cans cream of potato soup, undiluted
1 can cream-style corn
1 1/2 cups half-and-half
1 1/2 cups milk
2 bay leaves
1/2 tsp. garlic powder
Salt to taste
1/2 tsp. white pepper
2 dashes Tabasco sauce
1 pound lump crabmeat,

onto the monkey's buttocks. This hurt him so much that he cried, "Mr. Crab, please let me loose. If you will, I'll give you three hairs from my buttocks."

And that is why today there are hairs growing on the crab's scissor claws.

Sauté celery, green onion, and green pepper in butter until tender. Add potato soup, corn, half-and-half, milk, bay leaves, garlic powder, salt, pepper, and Tabasco. Cook until thoroughly heated and smooth. Gently stir in crabmeat and heat thoroughly. Remove bay leaves before serving.

SERVES 8

Maryland Cream of Crab Soup

½ cup cooked celery, diced
2 Tbls. butter
1 Tbls. flour
2 quarts milk
½ onion, minced
2 Tbls. chopped parsley
1½ tsp. salt
⅛ tsp. pepper
2 cups crabmeat
Whipped cream

Boil 2 or 3 stalks of celery in water until limp. Chop and measure one-half cup. In the top of a double boiler, melt the butter. Add flour and blend, stirring constantly until smooth. Add milk gradually, still stirring. Add onion, parsley, celery, salt and pepper. Cook slowly until soup thickens a little; add the crabmeat. Serve in individual dishes with a spoonful of whipped cream on top.

SERVES 8–10

East Coast Crab and Tomato Bisque

1 10-ounce can condensed creamy onion soup, undiluted
¾ cup skim milk
½ tsp. Worcestershire sauce

¼ tsp. dried basil
⅛ tsp. thyme
1 8-ounce can stewed tomatoes
½ pound crabmeat
Lemon slices for garnish
Fresh parsley for garnish

In large saucepan, combine soup, milk, Worcestershire sauce, basil and thyme; blend well. Stir in tomatoes. Bring to a boil on high heat. Reduce heat; simmer 5 minutes, stirring occasionally. Add crabmeat and heat 3 to 5 minutes longer. Garnish with lemon slices and fresh parsley, if desired.

SERVES 4

Carla Bayard's Creamed Corn and Crabmeat Soup

2 cloves garlic, minced
½ bunch green onions, minced
3 Tbls. butter
1 Tbls. flour
2 cups milk
2 cans whole kernel corn, with liquid
2 cans creamed corn
1 pound crabmeat
Tabasco sauce to taste
Salt to taste

Sauté garlic and green onions in the butter; add the flour and cook about 2 minutes, stirring constantly. Add the milk and cook a few minutes, still stirring constantly. Add the whole kernel corn and its liquid, the creamed corn, crabmeat, Tabasco, and salt. Simmer gently long enough to heat the crabmeat through (do not boil). (Note: if Zatarain's Liquid Crab Boil is available, use it instead of Tabasco for a much more interesting flavor. Use sparingly, a few drops at a time, then stir and taste.)

SERVES 6

Marie Mumme's Cream of Crab and Asparagus Soup

2 packages frozen asparagus
¼ cup butter or margarine
¼ cup flour
1 tsp. salt (or to taste)
⅛ tsp. ground nutmeg
⅛ tsp. white pepper
1½ quarts milk
1 pound crabmeat
3 cups sharp Cheddar cheese, grated
Paprika for garnish

Cook, drain, and chop the asparagus. Melt butter or margarine in a 4-quart saucepan; blend in flour, add salt, nutmeg, and pepper. Gradually add milk, stirring constantly; cook until mixture is thickened and smooth, still stirring constantly. Add crabmeat, asparagus, and cheese and continue to stir until cheese melts. Garnish with paprika and serve hot.

SERVES 12

Cioppino

Cioppino (pronounced "cha-PEE-no") is a San Francisco Italian-style specialty. This tomato-based hot crab soup has been popular on the West Coast since the Italian immigrants arrived in San Francisco back in the 1800s. Many of the Italian families moved up the coast and settled in small fishing villages in northern California and Oregon where they opened restaurants. This soup should be served with lots of good, hot sourdough French or Italian bread for dunking, and some bibs or large cloth napkins.

2 lbs. striped bass or rock cod
½ pound raw, peeled shrimp
2 big Dungeness crabs, cooked, cleaned, and quartered
1 large onion, chopped
¼ cup olive oil
1 tsp. minced parsley
1 clove garlic, minced
3 cups canned or fresh tomatoes, chopped
½ cup chopped celery
Salt and pepper to taste

Clean the fish, cut into serving-sized portions, and arrange in a large kettle. Add shrimp and crabs. In another pan, brown onion in olive oil; add parsley and garlic and cook 5 minutes. Stir in tomatoes, celery, salt and pepper; cook 10 minutes. Add to kettle with seafood and cook slowly about 30 minutes. Serve in soup plates giving a selection of each kind of seafood and some sauce. Serve with bib, bread, and lots of napkins.

SERVES 12

Cioppino Variations

Add clams or mussels in the shells to the above seafood. Add fresh vegetables such as chunks of zucchini squash, eggplant, or potatoes together with 1 clove of minced garlic. Sauté the vegetables in 3 cups of fresh tomatoes and 1 cup of white or red dry wine.

Cioppino No. 2

½ cup olive oil
2 bunches green onions, diced
2 large onions, chopped
2 green peppers, diced
4–6 cloves garlic, crushed
2 cups dry wine
1 28-ounce can tomato puree
4 cups water
2 bay leaves
1 tsp. oregano
1 tsp. basil
⅔ cup chopped parsley
1 Tbls. salt
1 Tbls. sugar
2 large Dungeness crabs cooked, cleaned and broken into
  quarters
2 dozen unshelled clams
2 dozen large raw shrimp, peeled
2 pounds black sea bass, cut into large chunks

Heat oil in Dutch oven. Add onions, peppers and garlic; sauté for 5 minutes. Add wine; simmer for 15 minutes. Add tomato puree, water, bay leaves, oregano, basil, parsley, salt, and sugar; simmer for 1 hour. Clean and crack crabs; place in large kettle. Top with clams. Arrange shrimp on top of clams. Place fish on top of shrimp. Add hot sauce; cover. Simmer for 20 to 30 minutes or until clams open. Serve with hot bread for dipping, bibs, and napkins.

SERVES 12

Italian-Portuguese Crab Stew

1 bunch green onions, chopped
1 large clove garlic, minced

1 bunch fresh parsley, chopped
2 large cans tomato sauce
½ cup cooking oil
1 tsp. Accent
1 tsp. cumin
1 tsp. whole cloves
3 dry chili peppers
½ cup dry red wine
6–7 quarts water
6 large Dungeness crabs, cleaned, cooked and cracked
Bread sliced in thick pieces

Combine all ingredients except wine, crabs, and bread. Cook in an 8-quart kettle until consistency is similar to spaghetti sauce. Add wine; simmer for 30 minutes. Add water and bring to a boil. Add freshly cooked crabs with shells. Simmer for 45 minutes to 1 hour. Place slice of bread in individual soup dishes; pour whole cracked crab and sauce over bread.
SERVES 12

Creole Barbecued Crab Bisque

1 large onion, chopped
4 stalks celery, chopped
3 cloves garlic, minced
1 cup tomato juice
4 peppercorns
2 cups chicken consommé
1 bay leaf
2 Tbls. Worcestershire sauce
4 Tbls. salad oil
1 sprig parsley, minced
4 Tbls. soy sauce
3 cups crabmeat

Sauté onion, celery, and garlic in oil. Add remaining ingredients except soy sauce and crabmeat. Cover and simmer for 30 minutes. Strain and add soy sauce. Cook crabmeat in the barbecue sauce for 20 minutes. Serve with hot bread for dipping.

SERVES 6

Main Dishes & More

The Blue Crab

The Crabbing Industry

Native American Folklore

Greek Folklore

Cajun Crabmeat-Filled Crepes

Crepes
³/₄ cup milk
²/₃ cup flour
3 eggs, beaten
¹/₂ tsp. salt

Filling
4 Tbls. butter or margarine
1 cup sliced mushrooms
¹/₄ cup sliced green onions
¹/₄ cup flour
1¹/₂ cups milk
¹/₄ cup dry white wine
1¹/₂ cups shredded Swiss cheese
¹/₂ pound crabmeat

The Blue Crab

The first part of the scientific name for the blue crab, *Callinectes sapidus*, means beautiful swimmer, which is a more accurate label than "blue" for this many-colored crustacean. The blue crab is also dark green, blue-green, or brownish on the top with a whitish, cream color underside, with dark blue, red, fuchsia, or orange markings on the legs and chelipeds. It is a member of the decapod family of Portunidae, the swimming crabs, in which the last pair of walking legs were modified into flat, swimming paddles.

The beautiful swimmer is migratory and travels over large areas during its lifetime. In the United States, this cold-blooded crab is found on muddy bottoms in shallow waters all the way from Cape Cod to Texas. It even strays as far north as Nova Scotia and as far south as Uruguay.

Seen sporadically in Denmark, Holland, and France, the blue crab in recent years has also appeared in the Mediterranean, where it has proliferated in Greece's Aegean Sea. It is now an established resident along the coasts of Egypt and Lebanon as well, having probably hitched a ride from America in the bilges of ships.

Blue crabs appear inshore in the warm weather months, as early as February in Louisiana. They stay in the shallows until winter's chill winds blow. They spawn from May to October in the Gulf of Mexico or to the east in the Atlantic Ocean.

The female blue crab has a lot of aliases. She is known in folk speech as a "sponge crab," "cushion crab," or "berried crab," when she is carrying eggs, and a "ballie," "busted sook," "orange crab," "punk," and "lemon crab" after she has released her eggs.

With its stalked, compound eyes, the feisty blue crab perceives movements and responds with quick thrusts of its chelipeds. Chelipeds are the two large, powerful claws that are used to seize and crush the prey, tear it apart, and guide it to the mandibles where it is eaten.

The chelipeds are also responsible for many minor injuries to inexperienced crabbers. If you should ever

¼ cup chopped pimento
½ tsp. dry mustard
½ tsp. salt
⅛ tsp. paprika

To make the crepes, combine milk, flour, eggs, and salt; beat until smooth. Let stand at room temperature for 30 minutes. For each crepe, pour 3 to 4 tablespoons batter into hot, lightly greased, 7-inch crepe pan or skillet, tilting and turning pan to coat with batter. Cook until lightly golden. Remove and keep warm. In saucepan, brown mushrooms and onions until tender in butter. Add flour and cook, stirring until bubbling. Remove from heat and stir in milk. Cook, stirring until liquid is thickened and smooth. Add wine and 1 cup of the cheese. Stir until melted. Add crab, pimento, mustard, salt, and paprika. Use to fill crepes. Roll up and place crepes in shallow baking dish, about 12- × 8- inches. Sprinkle with remaining cheese and bake at 350° for 20 minutes or until hot and bubbling.

MAKES 12 crepes

California Crab Enchiladas with Salsa

2 Tbls. peanut oil
8 corn tortillas
1½ cups crabmeat
1 cup sour cream, divided
Small jar salsa, mild or medium, divided
¼ red onion, minced
½ tsp. salt
¼ tsp. white pepper
½ cup Monterey Jack cheese, grated
1 green onion, sliced

Heat peanut oil in heavy skillet. Quickly heat tortillas in oil, allowing a few seconds each. Drain on paper towels. Mix crabmeat with ½ cup sour cream, ¼ cup salsa, and minced onion. Blend well, season to taste with salt and pepper, and set aside. Spread a thin layer of salsa in bottom of baking dish large enough to hold 8 rolled enchiladas. Place each tortilla on flat surface and put 2 heaping tablespoonfuls of crab filling down the middle. Roll up the tortilla and place seam side down in baking dish. Spread remaining salsa over enchiladas. Mix grated Monterey Jack cheese with remaining ½ cup sour cream and put a dollop on each enchilada. Sprinkle chopped green onion over top. Bake in preheated 375° oven for 25 minutes. Serve immediately.

MAKES 8 enchiladas

Mexican-American Microwave Crab Enchiladas

This recipe requires a 4-cup glass measuring cup and a 7- x 11-inch glass baking dish.

Sauce

2 Tbls. margarine
1 cup chopped onion
1 10-ounce can Ro-tel tomatoes and green chilies, chopped
1 8-ounce can tomato sauce
1 tsp. chili powder
½ tsp. oregano
½ tsp. salt

Put margarine in measuring cup and melt with oven on HIGH for 30 seconds. Add onion and sauté on HIGH for 3 minutes. Add tomatoes and green chilies, tomato sauce, chili powder, oregano and salt. Mix well. Bring to boil on HIGH for 2 minutes 30 seconds. Cover with a paper towel and microwave on HIGH for 4 minutes. Let stand, covered.

find some part of your anatomy suddenly attached to a crab's deft pincers, which only seconds before had seemed to be a safe distance away, try to remember the following advice, given by an expert crabber: DO NOT panic. Don't obey your instinct to fling the crab immediately away from you. That is what usually tears the skin, not the pincer. Bear with the pain until the crab lets go.

Besides, if you fling a blue crab into the air it can first rip your hand and then come down spike-first into your foot or some other soft, tender part of your anatomy. Furthermore, airborne blue crabs make very dangerous flying missiles, particularly if you have any crabbing partners nearby.

Safely picking up live blue crabs with the fingers requires nerve as well as technique. First, one should gently but firmly step on the crab to keep it from running away (preferably, one should be wearing shoes). Then, in most cases, it is safe to grab the crab from the back with the fingers in the center of the top shell and the thumb on the underside. However, some blue crabs appear to be double or even triple-jointed, and can reach around back and pinch the side of the hand!

A less dangerous way is to grab them by the two big spikes that protect their elbows. This method, however, requires real courage. An even safer way is to take a firm hold of the crab with the thumb and forefinger at the base of either one of its two paddle-shaped flippers.

The blue crab is a capable predator, armed and dangerous. It eats clams, mussels, and even other crabs. It does not like to eat rotten, stinky things, as many folks mistakenly believe. It senses water currents and nearby food sources through tactile and chemical receptors located on its double set of antennae. These whiskers constantly move jerkily in the direction of the approaching current. As they move, there is a rapid beating of the maxillipeds (small legs near the mouth), which force a current of water across the crab's head. This is how the crab, when underwater, can sense and smell its surroundings and respond quickly when danger—or food—is nearby.

Blue crabs are color coded

Filling

1 pound crabmeat
2 cups Monterey Jack cheese, shredded and divided
⅓ cup chopped ripe olives
12 soft corn tortillas
Dairy sour cream for topping

Combine crabmeat, 1 cup of the cheese, olives, and ½ cup of sauce. Mix well. Dip each tortilla in the warm sauce. Lay flat in greased 7- x 11-inch baking dish. Fill each tortilla with equal portions of crabmeat filling; roll and place seam side down. Spoon remaining sauce over top and sprinkle with remaining 1 cup cheese. Microwave on HIGH for 5 minutes. Rotate dish one time. Serve topped with sour cream, if desired.

MAKES 12 enchiladas

Creole Stewed Crabs

12 large, live blue crabs
1 large onion, minced
1 Tbls. butter
3 large cans tomatoes, chopped
1 stalk celery, chopped
Pinch (each) thyme and parsley
1 fresh bay leaf, minced
Salt and cayenne pepper to taste
1 garlic clove, minced
Rice or new potatoes

Boil the crabs for 5 minutes. As soon as they have cooled off, clean them and break them in half. Save the claws, cracked, for the stew. Sauté the onion in the butter until translucent; add the tomatoes and cook until brown. Stir in the celery, thyme, parsley, and bay leaf; add salt and cayenne pepper to taste. Add garlic and cook for another ten minutes, stirring occasionally. Then add the crabs and cook them ten minutes more. Serve over boiled white rice or peeled new potatoes boiled whole.

SERVES 6

Italian Crab and Rice

1 cup uncooked rice
1 garlic clove, minced
2 medium onions, chopped
3 Tbls. olive oil
2 8-ounce cans tomato sauce
Salt and pepper to taste
¹/₃ cup parsley, chopped
1 pound crabmeat
¹/₂ cup grated Parmesan cheese

Rinse the rice in a strainer. Drain. Sauté rice, garlic, and onions in olive oil until rice is translucent. Add tomato sauce, salt, and pepper; cover and steam until rice is done (about 15 minutes). Remove pan from heat and stir lightly to loosen rice. Add parsley, crabmeat and cheese. Stir well. Cook over a low heat until all ingredients are hot and the cheese has melted.

SERVES 6

King Crab Paella

1 10-to-12 ounce package frozen Alaska king crab split legs
1 clove garlic, minced
¹/₂ cup chopped onion
2 Tbls. olive oil
1 pound chicken breasts, skinned, boned, and cut into chunks
1 cup raw rice
¹/₄ pound smoked sausage, chopped

so they (and we) can tell the boys from the girls. Whereas mature male crabs have blue chelipeds, mature females have reddish-orange colorations that resemble nail polish on the tips of their chelipeds. The female crab also appears to be wearing "lipstick" on her underside. The oval, serrated plate located there sometimes has a reddish color on it that reminds some folks of lipstick on human lips. At least that's what the fishermen say. Of course, they might be the same type of guys that mistook manatees for mermaids.

The fuchsia-colored nail polish on the chelipeds of virgin females turns bright red after mating. This is the signal that the females are mothers-to-be. Between May and July, and again in September, many doubles or carriers are caught. These terms refer to a large, hard male crab carrying his soft, molting female partner.

Louisiana is one of the nation's leading producers of meat from blue crabs. The two most productive areas are the Barataria estuary, a huge, triangular coastal area well south of Baton Rouge, and Lake Pontchartrain, a large, brackish body of water on the north side of the city of New Orleans. The world-famous seafood dishes of Louisiana regularly feature crabmeat since it is so readily available and is less expensive than in other parts of the country.

A good many of the blue crabs caught in Lake Pontchartrain have migrated there all the way from the Chandeleur Islands in the Gulf of Mexico. These barrier islands lie to the south of the Mississippi towns of Pascagoula and Biloxi. Sponge or berried crabs, female crabs bearing egg masses under the abdomen, go there to lay their eggs because the water has a high salinity.

As many as seven hundred thousand to two million eggs are laid by a single female in one spawning! Afterwards, the females usually remain in the gulf waters, and in August, large numbers of the dead spent females are found on the beaches.

The hatchlings go through two larval stages that last just over a month, then transform into minuscule crabs one-tenth of an inch long. Only about one

1 tsp. salt
¼ tsp. pepper
½ tsp. oregano
Pinch of saffron, crushed
2 cups chicken broth
1 tomato, peeled and diced
¾ cup fresh or frozen peas
2 Tbls. sliced pimento
¼ cup chopped parsley

Thaw crab legs. Put the oil in a large heavy skillet. Over a low fire, sauté garlic and onion and when soft, push to one side of pan. Add chicken and brown, stirring often to keep onion and garlic from burning; remove from pan. Add rice to pan and stir over high heat until rice is lightly toasted. Return chicken to pan and add sausage, seasonings, and chicken broth. Bring to boil; simmer, covered, 20 minutes or until rice is tender. Carefully fold in crab, tomato, peas, and pimento; simmer, covered, 15 minutes longer. Remove cover from skillet and cook until all moisture is absorbed. Sprinkle with parsley. (Recipe courtesy Alaska Department of Fish and Game.)
SERVES 6

Marie Mumme's Crabmeat with Mushrooms and Wild Rice

1 7-ounce package long grain and wild rice
2 cups sliced fresh mushrooms
⅓ cup butter
1 tsp. salt
½ tsp. white pepper
1 pound crabmeat
2 Tbls. dry white wine
2 Tbls. fresh lemon juice

Cook rice according to directions. Add mushrooms 5 minutes before end of cooking time. In a hot skillet, melt butter and add salt and pepper. Stir in crabmeat, wine, and lemon juice. Cook about 3 minutes, stirring frequently, until crabmeat is heated thoroughly. Serve immediately over wild rice mixture.

SERVES 4–6

Creole Crabmeat and Rice Dressing

1½ cups raw rice
1 large onion, chopped
½ green pepper, chopped
1 celery stalk, chopped
1 stick margarine, melted
2 small jars mushrooms, drained
1 10-ounce can chicken broth
1 pound crabmeat
Salt and pepper to taste

Rinse the rice in a strainer. Sauté rice, onion, green pepper, and celery in the melted margarine until rice is translucent. Add the mushrooms, chicken broth, crabmeat, salt and pepper. Bring to a boil and cover; reduce heat and simmer for about 15 minutes or until rice is done.

SERVES 6–8

Florida Basic Blue Crab Stuffing

½ cup chopped onion
⅓ cup chopped green pepper
⅓ cup chopped celery
2 cloves of garlic, minced
⅓ cup margarine, melted

out of ten thousand of the larvae survive to become adults.

The baby crabs soon begin active predation and migrate through the tidal inlets into the lower entrances of estuaries in search of their own food and to avoid becoming somebody else's. To get into Lake Pontchartrain, some blue crabs swim and crawl a distance of almost 120 miles! The migration can take up to two years to complete for some full-grown adult males. (This fact gives new meaning to Fats Domino's hit song, "Walkin' to New Orleans"!)

During this long journey that takes many months to complete, the juvenile crabs grow and change their clothing frequently. Technically, the process is called ecdysis, but we know it as molting or shedding. It happens over and over again for growing crabs. The ones that will shed their shells in a day or two are called peelers.

When they get too big for their britches, the fat little crabs find that their shells start to crack. These buster crabs must squeeze and wiggle out of their old cracked shells and go about dressed in new, soft shells. Extremely vulnerable at this time, the buster crabs are very tasty since the shell is still quite soft.

Just a day later they become paper-shell soft crabs—still good to eat, but with shells that are a bit tougher. The soft crabs must hide and drink lots of water to get back to their original armored state. After about twenty-four hours the new shells have plumped out and hardened to the consistency of tough plastic.

Despite a Louisiana folk belief, intentionally breaking one of the claws off a hard-shell blue crab will not cause it to molt and turn into a soft-shell crab. All crabs have the ability to regenerate lost appendages. In order to escape capture, crabs are able to drop any appendage. The appendage will regenerate, sooner or later. So, the process of molting is a matter of the blue crab's size and internal rhythm, not the loss of a claw.

All soft crabs are vulnerable, but soft females in their final molt before sexual maturity are the most vulnerable of all. This is when they catch the compound eyes of the lustful adult

1 pound crabmeat
2 cups soft bread crumbs
2 eggs, beaten
1 Tbls. chopped parsley
1 tsp. salt
1/2 tsp. black pepper or Tabasco sauce to taste

Sauté onion, green pepper, celery, and garlic in the melted margarine until tender, not brown. Combine all ingredients and mix well. Makes enough stuffing for 6 small flounders or 1 very large flounder. Also may be used to stuff other fish, shrimp, steamed or boiled artichokes, boneless chicken breasts, veal or other meats. (Recipe courtesy of Florida Department of Agriculture and Consumer Services, Bureau of Seafood and Aquaculture.)

Creole Baked Stuffed Fish with Crab and Tomato Sauce

2 Tbls. chopped onion
2 Tbls. chopped celery
2 Tbls. chopped green pepper
1/4 cup plus 2 Tbls. butter, melted and divided
2 Tbls. flour
1/2 cup milk or cream
1/4 tsp. salt
1/8 tsp. paprika
2 drops Tabasco sauce
1/8 tsp. pepper
2 tsp. Worcestershire sauce
1 cup cooked crabmeat
1 cup cooked shrimp, chopped
1/2 tsp. chopped parsley
6 sole or halibut fillets
Tomato sauce

Sauté onion, celery, and green pepper in ¼ cup melted butter; cook until ingredients are soft but not brown. Stir in flour and milk and cook, continuing to stir until thickened; remove from heat. Mix in seasonings, crabmeat, shrimp, and parsley. Mound some stuffing on each fillet, roll up and secure with wooden picks; put roll-ups, leaving space between, into shallow greased baking dish. Brush fish with remaining melted butter. Bake at 350° for 15 minutes. Pour tomato sauce over top; return to oven and bake 25 minutes.

SERVES 6

Tomato Sauce

4 cups canned tomatoes
1 tsp. salt
½ tsp. thyme
1 garlic clove, minced
1 bay leaf, crumbled
Black and cayenne pepper to taste
2 Tbls. butter
1 Tbls. flour

Combine tomatoes, seasonings, and a tablespoon of the butter in a saucepan; boil over a medium heat until sauce is reduced to half, stirring occasionally. In another saucepan, melt remaining butter, blend in the flour and cook over a low heat until thick and smooth; mix with sauce and cook 5 minutes longer.

Louisiana Baked Crab-Stuffed Green Peppers

6 large green peppers
1 cup light cream
4 Tbls. butter
⅛ tsp. ground nutmeg

males, and when mating takes place.

Blue crab courtship is a spectacular ritual that not many humans have observed, since it takes place underwater. The males act very excited and get way up on their tiptoes while the females rock side to side. This is their way of signalling to each other that they are ready to mate.

A courting male first stands up high on his walking legs and then extends his arms (claws) in a straight line and begins to wave his swimming legs. To make certain he is not ignored, he snaps his body backwards and kicks up a storm of sand with his legs. The soon-to-be-mature female gets the message fast. She rocks back and forth, waves her claws in and out, and approaches the male, at which point she turns around and attempts to back under him.

The male then attempts the grab, whereby he seizes with his claws whatever part of the female he can reach and tries to put her in the cradle position. The female waves her arms helplessly, playing hard to get but not really trying to escape. Soon she quiets down and allows herself to be cradle-carried, right side up and face forward.

This stage lasts at least two days but may go on as long as a week before the female's last molt. During the molt, the male protects his little sweetheart by standing guard over her and making a cage with his walking legs. He does this very patiently, since her molt may take two or three hours. When at last she lies exhausted and glistening in her new skin, he lets her rest and drink the water she needs to plump out her body. Finally, the male gently helps the female turn herself over until she is on her back and is belly-to-belly beneath him.

When she is ready, the female opens her newly shaped abdomen to expose two genital pores. Into these the male inserts his pleopods (two small appendages underneath the tip of his elongated abdominal apron). When all is in place, the female extends her abdomen so that it folds around and over the male's back, preventing the risk of coitus interruptus. The blue crabs are now locked in love's embrace and may remain so for up to twelve hours!

2 Tbls. cornstarch
1/4 cup dry sherry
1 tsp. fresh lemon juice
Salt and pepper to taste
2 cups crabmeat
1 cup cooked white rice
Paprika for garnish

Cut the tops off the peppers and take out the seeds. Parboil them for 5 minutes. Drain upside down and let cool. Bring the cream to a boil, and add the butter and nutmeg. Mix the cornstarch, sherry, lemon juice, salt, and pepper. Add to the cream and cook until thick, stirring with a wire whisk constantly. Combine the mixture with the crabmeat and rice and spoon into the peppers. Sprinkle with paprika and bake in a greased baking dish for 20 minutes at 350°.
SERVES 6

Creole Baked Shrimp and Crab-Stuffed Green Peppers

8 to 10 medium green peppers
1 pound peeled shrimp, chopped
1 1/2 cups chopped onions
1 cup chopped celery
4 Tbls. light cooking oil
1 cup crabmeat
Salt and pepper
1 1/2 cups seasoned breadcrumbs
1 1/4 cups water

Cut tops off peppers, take out seeds, and parboil for 10 minutes. Drain upside down. Sauté shrimp, onions, and celery in oil until vegetables are tender; add crabmeat, season with salt and pepper and cook 5 minutes. Remove mixture from heat and gradually add the breadcrumbs. Stuff the peppers with this mixture. Put water in a baking dish, add peppers, and bake for 40 minutes at 375°.

SERVES 8–10

Creole Baked Crab-Stuffed Tomatoes

6 large, firm tomatoes
Salt and pepper to taste
3 Tbls. melted butter
1/4 cup minced parsley
1 Tbls. fresh lemon juice
1 pound crabmeat
1/4 cup grated Parmesan cheese
1/4 cup white bread crumbs

Wash tomatoes and remove the stem ends; scoop out the centers and save for another use. Sprinkle the tomatoes inside and out with salt and pepper. Mix the butter, parsley, lemon juice, and crabmeat. Fill the tomatoes. Mix the cheese and bread crumbs and sprinkle over the tops of the tomatoes. Place in a deep, well-greased baking dish. Bake at 350° for 20 minutes.

SERVES 6

Marie Windell's Crab in Zucchini Boats

4 medium zucchini, ends cut off
3 Tbls. olive oil, divided
1/2 cup minced onions
1 cup crabmeat
1/2 cup sour cream
2 tsp. Dijon mustard
2 Tbls. minced fresh parsley

After mating, the female is again cradle-carried by the male for at least forty-eight hours, during which her shell hardens and she regains some muscle tone. When she is finally let go, she rushes off with her prize: a male sperm packet that she will keep until the time is right. She must begin her journey back to the salty Gulf of Mexico waters where she will spawn and use the sperm packet to produce her little larvae.

Long ago, humans discovered that soft-shell blue crabs were exquisitely delicate-tasting morsels. Unlike soft-shell market crabs (such as the Dungeness), they are full of delicious meat. They are primarily eaten either fried in a light batter or broiled. The proper preparation of this unique delicacy does involve specific techniques. Please read the section on pages 86–87 on cleaning and preparing soft-shells before you cook them.

As a predator, the hard-shell beautiful swimmer eats a wide variety of seafood, catching many different types of fish in the waters of the Gulf of Mexico and Lake Pontchartrain, and digging up clams and mussels from muddy lake bottoms. Not infrequently crabs prey upon others of their kind. Most often hard crabs go after the soft ones. Fresh and decomposing vegetation also provide food.

Blue crabs are omnivorous, to a degree. As scavengers, they feed on fresh and decomposing flesh of all kinds. It must be kept in mind, however, that scavenging accounts for only a tiny percentage of the blue crab's regular diet. Blue crabs, and most crabs for that matter, are picky eaters (pun intended). They want fresh food that tastes good, just as we do. Any other idea is the result of more of the same old prejudice against crabs.

The Crabbing Industry

Commercial crabbing is an important business in the economies of many states in our nation. Let us consider these industries as they exist in Louisiana, Florida, Alaska, and the tri-state region of California, Oregon, and Washington.

1 Tbls. *minced fresh basil*
Salt to taste
White pepper to taste
2–3 *drops Tabasco sauce*
½ *cup ground almonds*
¾ *cup grated Gouda cheese plus more for topping*
2 tsp. *fresh lemon juice*
¾ *cup French bread crumbs plus more for topping*
1 *egg, beaten well*
1 Tbls. *Madeira wine*
¼ tsp. *paprika for garnish*

Blanch zucchini in boiling water, simmering for about 5 minutes after water comes back to a boil. Remove zucchini to cold water; when cool, cut in half lengthways. Sprinkle lightly with salt, turn peel side up and drain for 15 minutes; rinse and dry. Hollow out core of each zucchini half, chop coarsely, and set aside. Sauté onions in 2 tablespoons olive oil until translucent; do not brown. Add chopped zucchini cores and sauté until tender. Remove from skillet to bowl.

In skillet, cook crabmeat in the remaining tablespoon of oil over low heat until heated thoroughly. Mix together the sour cream, mustard, parsley, basil, salt, pepper, and Tabasco and add them to the zucchini-onion mixture, along with the crabmeat, almonds, cheese, and lemon juice. Add ¾ cup bread crumbs, mix thoroughly, then add the egg and the wine. The mixture should hold its shape in a spoon. Add a little cream or crumbs if necessary.

Arrange zucchini halves in a baking dish. Fill zuchini boats with crab mixture as stuffing. Mix 3 tablespoons bread crumbs and cheese (Swiss cheese may be substituted) for topping and sprinkle on each boat. Dust with paprika. Bake at 375° for about 20 to 25 minutes. Do not overcook. The zucchini should be tender but not soft.

SERVES 4

Creole Baked Crab-Stuffed Eggplant

4 medium eggplants
1 stick butter
6 chopped green onions
2 cloves garlic, minced
2 pounds raw shrimp, peeled
1 cup crabmeat
1/2 tsp. oregano
1 Tbls. minced parsley
Salt and pepper to taste
4 slices bacon, fried and crumbled
1 cup seasoned bread crumbs
1/2 cup grated American cheese

Parboil eggplants whole; cut in half lengthwise and scoop out pulp, being careful not to break skins. Heat butter and sauté onions and garlic; add eggplant pulp and cook for 20 minutes. Add shrimp, crabmeat, oregano, parsley, salt, and pepper. Cook 10 minutes; add crumbled bacon and enough seasoned bread crumbs to absorb liquids. Stuff eggplants with ingredients and sprinkle with cheese or top with breadcrumbs. If breadcrumbs are used, dot with small pieces of butter. Bake in a moderate oven, 350°, until cheese melts or breadcrumbs are golden brown.

SERVES 8

Caribbean Baked Crab-Stuffed Avocadoes

3 firm avocados
6 Tbls. garlic vinegar
2 Tbls. butter
2 Tbls. flour
1 cup scalded cream
Salt and white pepper to taste

Louisiana

The approximately nineteen hundred commercial crabbers in Louisiana almost never use the round, drop nets used by individuals. They rely on other devices that result in more crabs for the amount of energy and time invested. These fishermen catch blue crabs that are actively feeding.

In 1991, Louisiana's commercial crab catch was about fifty-one million pounds worth eighteen million dollars dockside. Louisiana produces 26 percent of the total harvest in the United States, making its fishermen some of the most productive in the nation. Total employment generated by the crab industry is estimated to be thirty-five hundred individuals, and the total retail value generated by the crab industry in Louisiana is approximately ninety-nine million dollars.

Crab fishing gear is divided into hard-crab and soft-crab types. Hard-crab fishermen use either a trotline with baits or crab pots. Louisiana prohibits the use of shrimp trawls for the exclusive catching of crabs. Both hard and soft crabs must reach the market alive.

Trotlines are baited, hookless lines that are placed on the bottoms of lakes and channels of estuaries. Each line is stretched out between two poles that hold the lines in place. Durable baits, usually beef lips and ears, are tied directly to the lines with slip knots. As the lines are raised from the water bottoms, the determined crabs generally do not escape, but instead cling tenaciously to their meals with their chelipods.

The crab fisherman needs a small motor boat with an outrigger on one side to raise the trotline from the bottom and knock off the crabs. In the past, a hand dip net was used to catch the crabs being knocked off the baits. Now there is a mechanized crab cage available that eliminates the dip net, permits the use of longer trotlines, and increases the daily catch.

The design of crab pots varies, but most are built of chickenwire. Each pot has a bait container in the bottom center. Some crab pots have an upper and a lower chamber, but these are uncommon now since they are very hard to empty without losing some crabs. The pots

1½ cups crabmeat
1 Tbls. drained capers
2 drops Tabasco sauce
6 Tbls. grated Cheddar cheese

Cut avocados in half lengthwise and remove pits. Do not peel. (Slice a small piece off the bottom of each half to keep it from tilting to one side.) Sprinkle each avocado half with 1 tablespoon vinegar and let stand for 30 minutes. Melt butter and blend in flour. Add scalded cream. Cook, stirring constantly, until smooth and thickened. Add salt, pepper, crabmeat, capers and Tabasco. Stuff avocados with crab mixture and sprinkle each with a tablespoon of cheese. Arrange on a shallow, round baking dish or pie pan. Bake in preheated oven at 375° until thoroughly heated, about 20 minutes.

SERVES 6

Mexican-American Microwave Crab-Stuffed Avocadoes

The following recipe requires 1 large glass bowl and 1 9-inch round shallow baking dish.

3 Tbls. margarine
1 cup chopped onion
¼ cup heavy cream
½ tsp. salt
⅛ tsp. cayenne pepper
⅛ tsp. paprika
½ pound crabmeat
¼ cup seasoned bread crumbs
3 ripe avocados at room temperature
Lemon slice
½ cup grated Cheddar cheese

Place the margarine in the bowl and melt it on HIGH for 1 minute. Add the onion and sauté for 5 minutes. Stir in cream, salt, pepper, paprika, crabmeat and bread crumbs. Cover with plastic wrap and microwave for 2 minutes. Let stand covered until ready to stuff avocados. Halve the avocados and remove the seeds but do not peel. (Slice off a small part of the bottom of each half to keep it from tilting to one side.) Rub avocadoes with the lemon slice to prevent darkening. Spoon crab mixture into avocados and sprinkle with cheese. Arrange the stuffed avocados in the shallow baking dish. Microwave on HIGH for 2 minutes. Serve hot. (Stuffed avocados may be microwaved in individual dishes on HIGH for 30 seconds each.)

SERVES 6

Soft-Shell Blue Crabs Preparation

This preparation should be used for all of the following soft-shell crab recipes.

The greatest care must be taken in preparing and cleaning soft-shell crabs. They should always be cleaned just before cooking so they won't lose their natural juices and delicate flavor. For highest quality, avoid purchasing crabs that are already cleaned. Soft crabs may be purchased fresh or frozen.

Freezing fresh soft crabs is very easy and produces excellent results. However, don't clean them before freezing. Simply rinse with cold water and wrap with freezer paper or plastic wrap, folding the legs and claws near the body.

To clean: first, rinse the crab carefully under cold water, removing all sand, but do not scald or blanch it, as this destroys the fine flavor completely. With scissors, snip off the face about ½ inch behind the eyes. With the tip of the scissors or with the fingers, remove the hard sand bag from behind the mouth.

Lift the back of the shell at its pointed ends and cut away the feathery gills on each side. Flip the crab over, and lift and

have two funnel-shaped entrances on the sides through which the hungry and unsuspecting crabs enter for a meal. Most of the crabs don't have the opportunity to "eat and run." The fishermen use painted plastic bottles or corks as floats in order to locate and identify their pots. A fisherman using crab pots can average a larger daily catch than the trotline crabber, and the work is a bit easier.

Soft-crab fishermen still need boats, but they use bush lines and crab shedding cars. Soft crabs are worth as much as three times more than hard crabs, which justifies the extra work involved in harvesting them.

Back in 1927 a swampdweller living along Louisiana's Lake Cataouatche discovered that peeler crabs were attracted to fresh willow branches that were placed in the lake to catch river shrimp and eels. When the branches were raised from the water, molting blue crabs were found inside the mass of branches. Later it was discovered that branches of the evergreen seria bush (a wax myrtle, *Myrica cerifera*) worked even better. Now, clumps of them are tied to the trotlines, more specifically called bush lines, for soft-shell crab harvesting.

Knowing when a hard-shell blue crab is about to shed requires skill in the reading of a "sign" along a faint line on the lower or feathered edge of the crab's next-to-last paddle-like finlet. To the savvy commercial crabber, the color of the sign determines in which of several large floating boxes the hard crab will be held. If the color is white, the crab is called a green crab and will shed in seven to ten days. If the sign is passing from white to pink, the crab is called a second. If the color is pink, shedding will take place in two days to one week, depending on the shade. If the sign is red, shedding may occur momentarily or at the most within two days, and this crab goes right into the buster box for the soft-shell crab market.

Both the green and buster crabs must be kept alive until the molting process is artificially completed. However, they can never be put in the same containers because the green crabs will eat the busters as soon as they get out of their old, tight-fitting shells.

snip off the apron from the bottom near the back end. Then rinse again in cold water and pat dry with a clean paper towel.

Place the crabs in a shallow bowl containing enough milk to cover them. Bend them and rub them with the milk so that it is well distributed. Soak the crabs in the milk for 15 to 30 minutes, turning frequently.

Cajun Fried Soft-Shell Crabs

3/4 cup flour
1/2 tsp. paprika
1/4 tsp. garlic powder
1/8 tsp. cayenne pepper
4 medium-sized soft-shell crabs
5 Tbls. butter

In a paper bag, combine the flour, paprika, garlic powder, and cayenne pepper. Shake well to mix. Place the crabs, one at a time, inside the paper bag in the seasoned flour. Shake the bag to coat the crab. For an extra thick coating, dip the crab again in milk and shake again in the flour. Melt the butter in a heavy skillet over a medium-high heat. Sauté the crabs, two at a time, for about 3 minutes per side or until they are a delicate golden brown. Drain on a piece of brown paper that has been heated, either in the oven or in the microwave.

SERVES 2–4

New Orleans Soft-Shell Crabs Amandine

4 fried soft-shell crabs
1/2 cup sliced almonds
1 Tbls. lemon juice
Lemon wedges

Cook the crabs as in the above recipe for Fried Soft-Shell Crabs and place them on a heated platter in the oven to keep warm. Add almonds and lemon juice to the pan juices and sauté until the almonds are golden. Pour the almonds and the pan juices over the crabs. Serve with lemon wedges.

SERVES 2–4

New Orleans Soft-Shell Crabs Pontchartrain

4 fried soft-shell crabs
1/2 stick margarine
2 Tbls. cornstarch
1 cup milk
1/2 cup Cheddar cheese, cubed
1/8 tsp. white pepper
1 Tbls. chopped green onions
Parsley for garnish

Cook the crabs as in recipe for Fried Soft-Shell Crabs and place in the oven on a large platter to keep them warm. Melt the margarine in a saucepan. Stir in the cornstarch. Remove from heat; mix in the milk, cheese, pepper, and green onions. Return to medium heat, stirring constantly until sauce begins to boil and thicken. Pour over the crabs and garnish with parsley. (Note: for a variation on this sauce, delete the cheese and add sautéed shrimp.)

SERVES 2–4

Creole Broiled Soft-Shell Crabs

1 dozen soft-shell crabs
4 tsp. sifted flour
Butter

A special box called a shedding car was invented for use in the soft-shell crab industry. These handmade, cypress wood boxes are usually eight feet wide by twelve feet long by four feet high. They have heavy, tight-fitting lids to keep their prisoners from escaping. They are kept submerged in the shallow waters near the shore of Lake Pontchartrain or in the Barataria estuary.

Soft-shell crabbing is a cross between fishing and farming. It is hard, wet, and tricky work, but is worth it for the extra value of the resulting crabs. The shedding cars must be lifted and checked regularly, often four times a day, in a search for the new busters that have come out of their cracked shells to become soft-shell crabs.

To be above the legal size limit, the busters must measure four inches across the shell. A counter is a prized soft-shell crab larger than five and a half inches across. The production of one hundred counters a day is considered very good work for the soft-shell crabber.

Florida

Florida is the United States leader in stone crab production, averaging over four million pounds of claws. This is 99 percent of the nation's annual production. Cedar Key, Everglades City, Crystal River, the Florida Keys, and several historic Florida Gulf Coast communities owe much of their development to the stone crab industry.

In the early years the fishery was conducted from shore or from small boats, and traps were rarely set deeper than thirty feet. In the 1960s the fishery underwent major development when large vessels started fishing deeper waters. Most stone crab landings take place between Key West and Panacea, with the majority in Florida Bay.

Stone crabs are harvested with traps made of wooden or plastic slats. Claws that meet the legal limit are twisted off; the crab is then released back into the water to regenerate new harvestable claws called retreads, a process that takes about eighteen months. It is legal to remove one or both of the powerful blacktipped claws

Parsley for garnish
Lemons cut in quarters

Clean and prepare the crabs according to instructions given in Preparation, above. Coat them lightly with the flour, and brush the shells with a little melted butter or place a pat of butter on top of each shell. Place them beneath the broiler (not too close to the fire) and broil until a delicate brown color, generally about 15 minutes. Serve on a platter garnished with parsley sprigs and lemon cut in quarters. For a richer taste, pour a little melted butter with lemon juice and chopped parsley over the broiled crabs.

SERVES 6

Louisiana Deep-Fried Soft-Shell Crabs

4 soft-shell crabs
3 egg whites
Cold water
All-purpose flour seasoned with salt, pepper, and cayenne
*   pepper*
Oil for deep-frying

Clean the crabs according to instructions in Preparation, above. Prepare the batter by whisking the egg whites with an equal amount of cold water. Mix the flour and seasonings and sift. Dip the crabs in the egg white batter; drain. Lightly dredge them in the seasoned flour and shake to remove excess. Deep-fry at 375° for about 3 minutes until crabs are lightly browned and crispy. Turn crabs often while cooking. Drain on brown paper that has been heated in the oven or the microwave.

SERVES 2–4

Louisiana Soft-Shell Crabs Fried in Beer Batter

1 12-ounce can warm beer
1 cup all-purpose flour
2 tsp. salt
½ tsp. baking powder
1 tsp. paprika
6 soft-shell crabs
Oil for deep-frying

To mix batter, pour beer into bowl, then add flour and remaining ingredients. Mix well. Batter should be prepared at least 1 to 2 hours in advance since it will thicken as it stands. Clean crabs according to the instructions in Preparation, above. Dust the crabs lightly in flour, then dip one at a time in the batter. Deep-fry at 375° for about 2 to 5 minutes, depending on the size of the crabs. Turn them often while frying. Drain on brown paper that has been heated in the oven or microwave and serve immediately.

SERVES 3–6

Creole Fried Soft-Shell Crabs Louise

6 soft-shell crabs
1 egg
1 cup evaporated milk
1 tsp. Tabasco sauce
1 Tbls. McCormick's fried chicken seasoning
All-purpose flour
Lemon slices
Parsley, chopped
Oil for deep-frying

if the length of the forearm measures two and three-quarter inches. (Taking both claws from the stone crab may be legal, but it leaves the crab in a defenseless situation which it will not likely survive. The law should be changed to make this illegal.)

During the life of a stone crab, the same appendage may be regenerated three or four times. It is illegal in Florida to harvest whole stone crabs and the ecologically sound practice of declawing and releasing crabs makes the fishery self-perpetuating.

Since whole crabs may not be taken, only the claws are marketed. Freezing or icing raw stone crab claws causes the meat to stick to the inside of the shell. For this reason, the claws are cooked immediately upon landing and are always sold cooked, either refrigerated or frozen.

The cooked claw meat of the stone crab is large, rich, sweet, and firm in texture. Because the meat is so rich, a serving of three claws per person usually suffices. It makes an attractive appetizer served simply in its cracked shell.

Most people are purists when it comes to Florida stone crabs and prefer to eat them cold or steamed just long enough for reheating. They are very good with a mustard sauce. The cooked claw meat can also be picked from the shell and used in any recipe calling for cooked crabmeat. About two and a half pounds of cooked stone crab claws are required to yield one pound of crabmeat.

Florida's other important crab fishery is blue crab. With an annual output of over sixteen million pounds, the state is a substantial national producer. The earliest documented commercial fishery for blue crabs was in the Apalachicola area in the 1880s when crabs were caught on baited trotlines and were bartered for farm products. Crab-picking operations began in Apalachicola in 1930.

Alaska

Historically, the red king crab (*Paralithodes camtschatica*) was Alaska's top shellfish, but by 1984 the fishery had crashed, with the harvest down sixty-fold. The result was that Alaska completely closed the

Clean the crabs according to instructions in Preparation, above. Beat together egg and milk; season with Tabasco sauce and chicken seasoning. Soak crabs in this mixture in the refrigerator for 1½ hours. Roll crabs in flour and fry in deep fat fryer for 20 minutes or until reddish brown. Garnish with lemon slices and chopped parsley.

SERVES 3–6

Cajun Soft-Shell Crab Jambalaya

8–10 soft-shell crabs
Oil for frying
1 cup chopped onions
1 medium green pepper, chopped
Garlic powder to taste
Black pepper to taste
4 cups raw rice
8 cups water
2 Tbls. parsley flakes
Salt to taste

Clean crabs according to the instructions in Preparation, above. Cut in half. Cook onions in thick pot with very little cooking oil, adding green pepper, garlic powder, and black pepper, and stirring until onions are well browned. Put in soft-shell crabs and cook with onions until they start browning, adding a little water. When crabs are cooked (about 10 minutes), add rice and 8 cups of water; stir well. Add parsley and salt and stir once more. Cook on medium fire until rice starts boiling; then reduce heat, cover, and cook over very low heat for about 15 minutes or until rice is done.

SERVES 10–12

Greek-American Grilled Soft-Shell Crabs

6 soft-shell crabs
3 Tbls. fresh lemon juice
1/2 tsp. grated lemon rind
1/2 cup butter, melted
2 Tbls. minced parsley

Clean crabs and soak them in milk according to instructions given in Preparation, above. Remove and dry with a paper towel. Place crabs on a charcoal grill. Combine lemon juice and rind, butter, and parsley and baste crabs liberally and often while grilling them over a low heat about 12 inches from the coals. Grill for about 4 to 5 minutes on each side.

SERVES 3–6

Crab Omelette for Two

2 Tbls. butter or margarine
3 green onion tops, minced
1 small jar sliced mushrooms
1/2 cup chopped artichoke hearts
1/4 cup half-and-half
6 eggs, beaten until foamy
1/2 cup crabmeat
Salt and white pepper to taste

Melt the butter and lightly sauté the green onions. Add the mushrooms and artichoke hearts and cook for 2 minutes. Add the half-and-half to the beaten eggs, and pour this mixture over the vegetables. Add the crabmeat, spreading it evenly over the pan. Add salt and pepper to taste. Cook until brown on the bottom; turn and continue cooking until done. A mild cheese may be grated and added to this recipe for more richness.

state's four most productive areas.

Research eventually showed that the culprit was not over-fishing, as was first suspected, but was the warmer ocean environments that increased fish predation. The blue king crab fishery suffered a similar decline. Red and blue king crab populations remain depressed and may take another ten years or even longer to recover. To survive, Alaskan fishermen turned their attention to another crab species.

The golden king crab (*Lithodes aequispina*) was discovered to exist in vast numbers in waters between three hundred and three thousand feet, a much deeper habitat on the average than that of the red and blue king crabs. A new Alaskan Gold Rush has resulted, this one occurring in darkness, deep on the ocean floor, where four- to nine-pound, eight-legged nuggets are being captured and brought to the surface.

In the six-year period between 1982 and 1988, sixty-eight million pounds of golden king crab worth two hundred million dollars were harvested, and the bulk of this catch came from the Aleutian Islands.

King crabs are most commonly fished in large steel-framed and nylon-webbed king crab pots weighing between six hundred and seven hundred pounds. Each pot is baited, usually with chopped herring, then soaked for two days on the bottom before being lifted onto the boat by powerful hydraulic systems. The boats, between forty and two hundred feet in length, primarily fish in the Bering Sea.

King crab fishing can be very dangerous because of the presence of heavy pots and coils of line, the long hours, and seas that sometimes exceed twenty feet. Only male crabs can be legally sold, and the minimum size limits vary by species.

King crabs are delivered live to the canneries where they are cleaned, the result being two sets of legs (each called a section). The sections are cooked in boiling salted water, then dipped in cold salted water. They are frozen and shipped mainly to American and Japanese restaurants. Individuals then clean the crabs a second

West Coast Individual Crab Omelettes

1/2 pound frozen Alaska King crab
1 10-ounce package frozen green peas, cooked
1 10-ounce can white sauce
9 eggs
1/2 cup water
1 tsp. salt
1/4 tsp. pepper
Butter

Drain and slice crab. Combine with cooked peas and white sauce. Heat slowly. To prepare omelettes, beat eggs, water and seasonings until light and foamy. Preheat griddle to 300 to 325°. Brush entire surface with butter. Slowly pour 1/4 cup of egg mixture onto the griddle for each omelette, allowing it to spread. When omelettes are set and lightly brown on bottom, place 3 to 4 tablespoons of hot crab filling in center of each. Fold over with narrow spatula. (Recipe courtesy Alaska Department of Fish and Game.)

MAKES 12 omelettes or 6 servings.

Japanese Crab Omelette

2 ounces canned bamboo shoots
2 ounces fresh mushrooms
1/2 leek (use the white part)
5 eggs
1/2 tsp. salt
1 tsp. sake*
1 tsp. sugar
2–3 drops soy sauce
1/4 pound crabmeat
10 gingko nuts (canned)
Oil for frying

Slice the bamboo shoots and mushrooms and cut the leek in diagonal slices. Break the eggs in a bowl and mix in the salt, sake, sugar, and soy sauce. Add crabmeat and ginko nuts and mix well. In a skillet, heat plenty of oil. Pour in all the ingredients and fry. When about half cooked, turn over with a pancake turner and fry on the other side.

*Sake, Japanese rice wine, is available at Oriental markets, liquor stores, or specialty stores.

SERVES 2

New Orleans Angel Hair Pasta with Crabmeat

16 ounces angel hair pasta
½ stick butter
2 cloves garlic, minced
½ pound crabmeat
1 cup half-and-half
⅛ tsp. black pepper
½ cup grated Parmesan cheese

Cook pasta according to package directions until al dente; drain, cover, and keep warm. Heat butter and garlic in skillet and cook over medium heat until garlic is light brown. Add crabmeat, half-and-half, and pepper. Heat about 3 minutes, or until mixture begins to bubble, stirring occasionally. Add Parmesan cheese; stir for 1 minute. Remove from heat. Toss the crab sauce with the pasta. Serve immediately with extra Parmesan cheese.

SERVES 4

time and boil or steam the legs in either salted or unsalted water for twenty to thirty minutes. The crabmeat may be eaten either hot or cold, plain or with butter and garlic or seafood sauce. The crabmeat may also be used in salads, sandwiches, and various other dishes. Some people prefer to split the legs and broil them.

California, Oregon, and Washington

The Dungeness crab (*Cancer magister*) is the largest edible true crab. In Alaska and elsewhere it is known affectionately as the Dungee. Some weighing as much as five pounds and measuring up to ten inches across the top shell have been caught on the Oregon coast. Such a crab contains about one and a quarter pounds of meat, or just about enough to feed two hungry crab lovers!

Second in fishery size only to the blue crab, the annual average production of the Dungeness crab is 35 million pounds in California, Oregon and Washington. The 1991 catch for the Tri-State Region measured 27 million pounds. The total value of the tri-state Dungeness crab harvest ranged from four and a half to eighteen million dollars in the years between 1981 and 1991.

Dungeness crabs are found to some extent in nearly all the coastal estuaries and out to depths of 1,080 feet off shore, although most ocean crab is found in three hundred feet of water or less.

Commercial production fluctuates on a somewhat cyclical basis over a seven-to-ten-year period, with the catch ranging from as low as sixteen to over thirty-five million pounds. The precise causes of these fluctuations are not known, but they are believed to be environmentally related rather than fishery caused. Higher-than-average sea water temperatures, sometimes associated with the *el niño* phenomenon, are often cited.

The Dungeness crab fishery had its beginnings in the San Francisco Bay area in 1863 with the first recorded commercial landings. By the 1880s, a substantial fishery existed there, and hoop nets were in use. The annual catches continued to increase and peaked at around two thousand metric tons in 1904.

New Orleans Angel Hair Pasta with Crabmeat No. 2

8 ounces angel hair pasta
2 Tbls. butter or margarine
1/4 cup olive oil
1/2 cup sliced green onions
1 garlic clove, minced
2 medium tomatoes, peeled, seeded, and chopped
1/4 cup dry white wine
1 Tbls. fresh lemon juice
1/2 cup crabmeat
1/2 cup chopped fresh parsley
Salt and pepper to taste

Cook pasta in large kettle of boiling water until al dente. Drain well and keep warm. Put butter and oil in heavy skillet over medium heat. Add green onions, garlic, tomatoes, and wine. Cook, stirring, until mixture boils. Boil gently for 2 minutes. Mix lemon juice, crabmeat, and parsley. Cook, stirring gently, just until crab is heated through. Season to taste with salt and pepper. Spoon sauce over pasta. Lift and mix pasta gently.

SERVES 2

Japanese Crabmeat Tempura

1 egg, slightly beaten
1/2 cup flour
1/2 cup water
2 cups peanut oil
1 pound Alaskan king crabmeat, cut into chunks

Make a batter of the egg, flour, and water. Heat oil to 370°. Dip the crabmeat chunks in the batter and cook them in the hot oil until brown. Drain on a paper towel. Serve with the piquant sauce, below.

SERVES 2

Piquant Sauce

½ cup hot chicken bouillon
2 Tbls. soy sauce
1 tsp. sugar
1 tsp. horseradish
½ tsp. monosodium glutamate (optional)

Mix the ingredients well. The piquant sauce should be served in tiny bowls into which the pieces of crab are dipped.

Creole Fried Hard Crabs

12 boiled large blue crabs
2 tsp. salt and 2 tsp. pepper, mixed together
1 pint milk
1 cup oil or shortening
2–3 cups stale bread crumbs
Parsley for garnish

Take the boiled crabs and remove the claws and crack them; clean the crabs and cut them into quarters. Sprinkle them liberally with the salt and pepper mixture. Put the milk in a wide, shallow bowl and have ready. Prepare a skillet of very hot oil and a plate of stale bread crumbs. (Seasoned or Italian bread crumbs may be substituted.) Dip the crabs into the milk and then roll them in the bread crumbs and drop them into the hot oil, frying about 10 minutes or until the crabs are a golden brown. Serve on a platter with the claws arranged in the center and the fried crabs grouped around them. Garnish with sprigs of parsley.

SERVES 6

However, some early indications of declining and fluctuating catch rates in the San Francisco vicinity resulted in the passage of significant crab conservation legislation at the state level. Possession and sale of female crabs was prohibited in 1897; a two month closed season was enacted in 1903; and a minimum size limit became the law in 1905. These regulations were not enough, however, to reverse the decline of crabs in the bay area. The Dungeness crab fishery first collapsed there in the 1920s, and again in the late 1950s. The bay area still has not recovered since 1960.

Strict conservation laws that affect Dungeness crab harvesting in the tri-state area continue into the present. The laws vary slightly from state to state; Oregon's laws will be used as an example here.

In Oregon, sport crabbers are limited to twelve male crabs daily. Each crab must be larger than five and three-quarters inches across the carapace (back shell), not counting the points. These big crabs are called keepers (as in finders-keepers, losers-weepers). Special bright yellow plastic crab gauges are sold at sporting goods stores. These are a part of the standard crabbing equipment for conscientious crabbers. If a gauge isn't available, some sport crabbers use a dollar bill (lengthwise) as a substitute. It works just fine, being six and one-eighth inches long.

The sport crabber is also limited in equipment usage to no more than three crab nets OR three pots. Since nets are cheaper, lighter to carry, and can even be rented, they are more commonly used. Sport crabbers may not keep more than two daily catch limits of crabs in a live trap or live box (special containers that hold the live crabs underwater to keep them alive until the crabber wants them).

The law also states that Dungees may not be mutilated so that sex, size, or species cannot be determined before landing. In other words, they must be brought to shore in the same lovely shape they were in when they were caught. It is also unlawful to retain female Dungeness crabs from any Oregon waters.

West Coast Crab Coquille

2/3 cup dry white wine
1/3 cup water
1 sprig parsley
1 small onion, halved
1 pound Alaskan king crab
2 Tbls. butter
1/4 pound mushrooms, sliced
2 Tbls. flour
1 10-ounce can cream of chicken soup
1/3 cup heavy cream
2 Tbls. lemon juice
6 baked pastry shells

Combine wine, water, parsley, and onion; heat to boiling. Add crab and simmer 5 minutes. Drain, reserving 1 cup of the stock. Cut the crabmeat into small pieces. Melt the butter in a pan; add the mushrooms and brown lightly. Blend in flour; gradually add soup, cream, and lemon juice; cook, stirring constantly, until thickened. Gradually stir in the reserved wine broth. Gently fold in crab pieces. Spoon into pastry shells.
SERVES 6

Cajun Deviled Crab

4 Tbls. melted butter
2 Tbls. chopped onion
2 Tbls. flour
3/4 cup milk
1/2 tsp. salt
1 tsp. Worcestershire sauce
Pepper to taste
1 Tbls. lemon juice
1 egg, beaten

1 Tbls. chopped celery
1 pound flaked crabmeat
¼ cup bread crumbs

With 3 tablespoons of the butter in a saucepan, sauté onion until tender; blend in the flour. Add the milk gradually and cook until thick, stirring constantly. Add seasonings and lemon juice and mix. Stir a tiny amount of the hot sauce into the egg; then stir back into the sauce. Add celery and crabmeat and mix. Place in 6 well-greased crab shells or ramekins. Combine the bread crumbs and remaining butter and sprinkle over top. Place on a baking sheet. Bake at 350° for 15 to 20 minutes or until golden brown.

SERVES 6

Florida Deviled Crab

¼ pound mushrooms, sliced
4 Tbls. butter, divided
1 tsp. minced onion
2 Tbls. flour
1 cup milk
1 egg yolk
1 tsp. dry mustard
1 tsp. horseradish
3 Tbls. minced parsley
1 tsp. salt
Dash cayenne pepper
12 blue crabs, cooked and picked
2 Tbls. lemon juice
12 cleaned upper shells
½ cup fine bread crumbs

Sauté mushrooms in 2 tablespoons of the butter until tender; add minced onion and cook 1 minute longer. Blend in

Finally, the ocean waters off the Oregon coast are closed to the taking of Dungees from August 15 through November 30. This holds for both sport and commercial crabbers. They may, however, take crabs during this period from bays, estuaries, beaches, tidepools, piers, and jetties which are open all year.

Commercial crabbers have other restrictions in Oregon. As with the sport crabbers, only male crabs may be taken, but the size limit for them is higher: six and one-quarter inches instead of the five and three-quarters inches for the sport crabbers.

Commercial crab pots (which weigh about one hundred pounds and cost about one hundred dollars apiece) must have at least two escape ports that allow nearly all crabs under 6¼ inches to escape before the pot is raised to the surface. This accomplishes two things. First, it saves the fisherman a lot of time otherwise spent sorting his catch. Second, since male crabs under 6¼ inches are mature and able to reproduce (and females cannot be taken), this assures there will always be a spawning stock. And, of course, it leaves lots of legal male crabs for the hungry sport crabbers.

There are significant fines, in the hundreds of dollars, for the violation of the Dungeness crab conservation laws in Oregon. Even sport crabbers have been fined heavily for disregarding the rules. Commercial crabbers (fishermen) can have their entire catches confiscated if they are found in violation. Only chronic repeaters among the fishermen lose their commercial licenses, however. The Oregon Department of Fish and Wildlife has marine field labs all along the coast, and it is part of their responsibility to see that these important laws are obeyed.

The bait used to catch Dungeness crabs includes clams, squid, or fish, or a combination of these. Among the fish used for bait, oily types like shad and Spanish mackerel are said by some to be preferred by the crabs. Snapper is also a popular bait fish. However, these fish aren't always available, so other types of bottom-feeding fish are used year-round. These are known collo-

flour and add milk gradually, stirring until thickened. Add the egg yolk, mustard, horseradish, 2 tablespoons of the parsley, salt, and cayenne; blend well. Add the crabmeat and lemon juice. Fill the clean crab shells (or use ramekins if preferred) with the mixture. Melt remaining butter and mix with bread crumbs; top shells with crumbs and remaining parsley. Bake in a hot oven (400°) for 10 minutes or until well browned.

SERVES 6

Baltimore-Style Deviled Crab

3/4 cup white sauce
2 egg yolks, beaten
2 cups crabmeat
1 tsp. prepared mustard
1/2 tsp. lemon juice, plus more to taste added before serving
2 Tbls. dry sherry
Dash of cayenne pepper
1/2 cup cooked, sliced mushrooms
2/3 cup buttered bread crumbs
1 tsp. minced parsley

White Sauce
2 Tbls. butter
2 Tbls. flour
1/2 tsp. salt
1/8 tsp. pepper
1 cup milk

To make white sauce, melt the butter and blend in the flour, salt, and pepper. Add the milk gradually, stirring constantly, until mixture boils and thickens; cook 2 to 3 minutes longer. Add a tiny bit of the hot sauce gradually to the beaten egg yolks; then stir back into the sauce, stirring constantly. Add the crabmeat and heat through. Add the mustard, 1/2 teaspoon lemon juice, dry sherry, cayenne, and mushrooms. Mix well. Transfer to greased crab shells or buttered ramekins. Sprinkle lightly with buttered crumbs and parsley. Brown in hot oven (450°) for 5 minutes. Sprinkle lemon juice over the top and serve hot.

SERVES 4

Southern Deviled Crab

2 strips bacon
1 onion, chopped
½ cup chopped celery
½ cup chopped green pepper
1 8-ounce box Ritz crackers, finely crumbled
¾ tsp. black pepper
Salt to taste
¼ tsp. cayenne pepper
1 tsp. Worcestershire sauce
1 egg yolk, beaten
¾ cup milk
½ cup dry sherry (optional)
1 pound crabmeat
2 Tbls. butter

Preheat oven to 350°. Fry bacon, drain, and crumble; reserve drippings. Sauté onions, celery, and green pepper in drippings. In a large bowl, combine ¾ of the cracker crumbs with the sautéed vegetables. Add seasonings, egg yolk, milk, sherry, and crabmeat, mixing well with a fork. Pour into a 1-quart casserole, and top with remaining cracker crumbs. Dot with butter and sprinkle with crumbled bacon. Bake 30 minutes.

SERVES 4–6

quially as rock cod carcasses (even though they contain no cod fish), a catch-all term for about twenty-five different species of bottom-feeding fish.

Crab bait should always be fresh for the best results. For some unknown reason, people have a misconception that crabs like to eat rotten, smelly, or yukky things. People who use spoiled meat for bait won't catch many crabs, because crabs are picky eaters and like their food fresh. They are only scavengers when there is nothing else to eat and they are famished.

Crab Fishermen's Jargon
Nobody likes to be called "crabby." Oregon commercial crabbers prefer to be called fishermen, as Oregon woodsmen would rather be called loggers than lumberjacks. Words like crabbers and lumberjacks do have some negative connotations that these people prefer to avoid.

The same goes for the crabbers in the Chesapeake Bay region who call themselves watermen. Labels like fishermen and watermen are used in an effort to deflect the snickers and innuendoes that the term "crabber" might evoke.

Besides, the fishermen label is more or less accurate, since in Oregon most of these men also fish as well as crab for a living, especially in the two and a half months each year when the crab season is closed.

Amateur crabbers, however, are not spared the innuendoes and are called sport crabbers. Many of these are vacationing tourists, some of whom evidently enjoy the wordplay and even have the audacity to wear T-shirts that say: "I CAUGHT [pictures of 3 red crabs] ON THE OREGON COAST," or "I HAVE A [picture of a large crab] ATTITUDE."

Souvenirs such as these can be bought at the Sportsman, a sporting goods store on the Pacific Coast highway in Florence that also rents crab nets by the hour or the day and has a daily posting of the high and low tides. (The best time to go crabbing is at slack tide, either low or high. This is when the water is not coming in or going out. At slack, crabs can move easily without bucking strong tidal currents and seem to come

Creole Stuffed Crabs

5 Tbls. butter
4 large onions, minced
1 large green pepper, minced
1 cup minced celery
1 cup water
4 cups crabmeat
4 eggs, beaten
1½ cups bread crumbs
1 cup minced green onion tops
1 cup chopped flat parsley
Crab shells

In large, heavy pot, melt 4 tablespoons of the butter; add onions, green pepper, celery, and water all at once. Simmer on low heat, 30 to 45 minutes. Do not brown. Add crabmeat and simmer another ½ hour. Remove from heat and cool. Add eggs, 1 cup bread crumbs, onion tops, and parsley. Mix thoroughly. When the crab mixture is cool enough to handle, pack in buttered crab shells. Sprinkle with remaining bread crumbs; dot with remaining butter. Bake at 325° for 15 minutes.

SERVES 8

Creole Stuffed Crabs No. 2

6 slices stale bread
3 eggs
1 cup evaporated milk
1 cup chopped onions
½ cup chopped celery
¼ cup chopped green pepper
2 garlic cloves, minced
½ cup oil
½ tsp. Worcestershire sauce

1 pound crabmeat
Salt and pepper to taste
½ cup chopped green onions
1 Tbls. chopped parsley
Bread crumbs
12 crab shells

Break the bread into very small pieces. Beat together eggs and milk and soak bread in mixture. Sauté onion, celery, green pepper, and garlic in the oil until wilted. Add the Worcestershire sauce, crabmeat, salt and pepper; cook over medium heat about 15 minutes, stirring constantly. Add green onions, parsley, and the soaked bread pieces; mix well. Fill crab shells with the mixture; top with the bread crumbs. Bake 15 minutes at 375°.

SERVES 6

Creole Fried Stuffed Crabs

1 dozen boiled crabs
1 stick margarine
1 large onion, minced
½ green pepper, minced
2 garlic cloves, minced
1 stalk celery, minced
2 eggs
1 cup bread crumbs
Salt and pepper to taste
1 cup milk
1 cup cornmeal or flour
Oil for deep-frying

Clean and pick the boiled crabs, saving the top shells for stuffing. Melt the margarine and sauté the onion, green pepper, garlic, and celery until wilted. Add the crabmeat and cook until

more readily to the odor trail from the bait.)

Warner Pinkney, owner and operator of the Sportsman, knows a lot about sport crabbing and gives advice and information for free. So crab-loving tourists can get a lot more than just vulgar T-shirts at his store.

Among both sport and commercial crabbers of Oregon's wild and rocky Pacific coast, a number of interesting folk speech terms can be heard. In some cases, the outsider is left wondering: what in the world are these people saying? A few examples of this insider's vocabulary will help you out if you ever decide to go a-crabbin' in Oregon:

Bait jars: small, sturdy, perforated plastic containers with screw-on lids that are placed inside the crab pots. The jars are filled with squid and clams, and the bait stays fresh for a fairly long time in these jars (as opposed to hanging bait described below). The holes in the jars are big enough to let the smell out, but not big enough for the hungry crabs to get a hook on the clams. The result is crab frustration and capture. Fishermen say the Dungeness crabs aren't very smart (because they are easily tricked into the crab pots by the bait jars) but acknowledge that they do have a good sense of smell.

Bait boxes: perforated metal boxes with tight-fitting lids that hold fish pieces and other bait for the crabs. They attach to the bottoms of the crab nets used more often by amateurs.

Bait bags: woven bags of small-width mesh used to hold cockle clams or small fish like herring. Used mainly by sport crabbers, they are attached to each side of the top net ring with wire hooks so that they are held in the center of the net.

Berried: a female Dungeness crab with a bright orange, sponge-like mass of between seven hundred thousand to two and a half million new eggs. Egg color gradually changes to dark brown. Female Dungeness crabs become berried during October and November.

Wire bait holder: devices resembling the type of large safety pins probably used for Paul Bunyan's diapers when he was a baby. These heavy-duty

the mixture is brown. Remove from the stove and add one egg, well beaten, and the bread crumbs. Mix well and season to taste. Stuff the crab shells with the mixture. Beat the other egg into the cup of milk, then dip the stuffed crabs in this liquid. Roll them in the cornmeal (or flour, if preferred), and deep-fry them in oil preheated to about 375° until brown.

SERVES 6

Thai Fried Stuffed Crabs

5 large crabs
4 ounces black Chinese mushrooms
2 ounces long-grain rice, cooked
6 ounces peeled, chopped shrimp
1 onion, chopped
1 shredded carrot
6 water chestnuts, chopped
1 egg, beaten
½ tsp. cornstarch
½ tsp. salt
¼ tsp. ground black pepper
Oil for deep-frying
Parsley, green onions, and red chili peppers for garnish
Sweet-and-sour sauce

Cook, clean, and pick the crabs, saving the tops for stuffing. Chop the crabmeat finely. Soak mushrooms and rice in warm water in separate containers for 15 minutes. Drain rice; drain mushrooms, discard the stems and chop finely. Thoroughly mix crabmeat, shrimp, mushrooms, rice, onion, carrot, water chestnuts, egg, cornstarch, salt and pepper. Stuff the shells with the crabmeat mixture. Heat the oil for deep-frying to medium heat. Deep-fry the stuffed shells for 12 to 15 minutes or until golden brown. Drain on absorbent paper towels. Garnish with parsley, green onions, and red chili peppers. Serve with sweet-and-sour sauce purchased from a Chinese or Thai market.

SERVES 5–10

Cajun Stuffed Crabs with Shrimp

1 cup creamy onion salad dressing
1½ cups chopped onion
¼ cup chopped celery
¼ cup chopped green pepper
1 cup boiled shrimp, minced
2 jalapeño peppers, minced
1 can cream of mushroom soup
½ cup mayonnaise
1 cup cooked rice
1 Tbls. sweet pickle relish
2 cups crabmeat
4 green onions, minced
3 sprigs parsley, minced
Salt and pepper to taste
Tabasco sauce to taste
1 cup crushed potato chips
15 cleaned crab shells

Heat half a cup of the onion salad dressing in a large saucepan; add the onion, celery and green pepper. Cook, stirring constantly, until wilted. Add the shrimp and jalapeño peppers; lower heat and cook until the liquid is absorbed. Add the soup, mayonnaise, rice, pickle relish, crabmeat, green onions, and parsley. Season with salt, pepper, and Tabasco to taste. Mix well. Spoon mixture into crab shells or into a baking dish. Brush the top with the remaining half cup of onion dressing and sprinkle with the potato chip crumbs. Bake at 350° for 20 minutes or until browned.

SERVES 8–12

holders are necessary, due to the strong Pacific tide currents, to securely attach large fish carcasses to the bottoms of crab nets.

Back in Bay St. Louis, Mississippi, we just used big safety pins for our chicken neck bait. The amateur crabbers who use this type of bait are called "chicken-neckers" by Chesapeake watermen. That sounds even worse than sport crabber.

Backin' crabs: removing the top shell from the bottom, in order to clean the crab. This term is also used by professionals working in the crabbing industry.

Bugs: a rather negative term used by fishermen for Dungees or other crabs harvested on the Oregon coast. Crabs may look like bugs to some, but not to devoted crab lovers.

Corkin': a stealthy technique used by some fishermen to lure away crabs from a competitor's string of pots. According to Dannie Owens, a fisherman who owns and operates the Siuslaw Charters out of Florence, Oregon, "It's when you get as close as you can to another guy's string of pots without getting hooked. Then you set your hangin' bait, and if you have better smellin' bait than they do, then their crabs will come to your pots."

Crab feed: a traditional feast on the Pacific Northwest Coast that resembles, in some ways, the New England clambake. Family and friends get together for both social occasions and community fund-raisers to enjoy sharing the local bounty from the sea.

Crackin' crabs: cleaning the crab and/or removing the meat from it for sale or use in cooking. In the South, we call this pickin' crabs.

Hangin' bait: a whole rock cod carcass suspended from a stainless steel hook inside the crab pot. Fresh hanging bait is used to draw the crabs quickly into the pot, but it doesn't last very long and should be replaced frequently. The large, s-shaped hook is run through the eye of the fish carcass and is then suspended inside the crab pot.

Pullin' crab pots: raising the heavy (one hundred pounds when they are empty) wire crab traps used by Oregon fishermen from below the water to the surface. The beauty

Creole Crab Croquettes

2 Tbls. butter
2 Tbls. flour
1 cup milk at room temperature
1 clove garlic, minced
½ tsp. salt
¼ tsp. white pepper
Dash of nutmeg
½ pound crabmeat
2 hard-cooked eggs, chopped
1 egg, beaten
Cracker crumbs
Oil for deep-frying

Melt the butter in a saucepan until bubbling; gradually add the flour and stir constantly with a whisk. Slowly add the milk to make a cream sauce. Add the garlic, salt, pepper, nutmeg, and crabmeat. Mix well. Add the chopped eggs. Put the mixture in the refrigerator for about 2 hours, then shape into small balls. Roll them in beaten egg and cracker crumbs and deep-fry in oil until golden brown.

SERVES 2

Creole Crab Croquettes No. 2

3 Tbls. butter plus butter for frying
5 Tbls. flour, sifted, plus flour for dredging
1½ cups milk
Salt, cayenne pepper, and black pepper to taste
1 egg, beaten
Pinch of celery salt
1 tsp. minced onion
2 cups lump crabmeat
Mayonnaise
French bread crumbs

Melt 3 tablespoons of the butter, and slowly blend in sifted flour. Add the milk and cook, stirring constantly. Add salt, pepper, cayenne, egg, celery salt, and onion and cook until thick. Add the crabmeat and mix well. Chill for several hours. Form into round, flat cakes and dip in flour. Spread mayonnaise on each side and roll in bread crumbs. Brown in hot butter. Serve with lemon wedges.

SERVES 4

Cajun Crab Patties

2 large onions, chopped
Oil for frying
1 quart crabmeat
1/4 cup parsley, chopped
1/4 cup chopped green onion tops
2 cloves garlic, minced
Salt and pepper to taste
1/2 cup seasoned bread crumbs

Sauté onions in oil; when golden brown, add crabmeat. Stir slowly; add parsley, onion tops, garlic, salt, and pepper. Let cook for 5 minutes. Add bread crumbs and stir well. Form patties and place them on a cookie sheet and freeze. When frozen, fry in oil until golden brown. (They hold together better if frozen first.)

SERVES 8

Chinese Pan-Fried Crab Cakes

1/2 pound bean sprouts
1/2 cup bamboo shoots
1 onion
3 1/2 Tbls. peanut oil, divided

of pots, however, is that they can be left underwater until the bait runs out, because the crabs can't just "eat and run" the way they can if nets (rings) are used.

Pullin' rings: the same hard task with much lighter equipment. Rings, the folk name for West Coast crab nets, should be pulled at least every twenty to thirty minutes, depending on how fast the crabs are coming to the bait. With ring nets, the usual method is to let the gear "fish" for about ten minutes before it is pulled. Lifting the nets sooner doesn't give the crabs enough time to locate the bait. Waiting longer means the crabs will eat your bait, thank you kindly for a free meal, and move on.

Rings: open-top crab nets. These are large, heavy-duty, two-ring devices mainly used by sport crabbers. The top ring is thirty inches in diameter; the bottom ring is twenty-six inches. A pulling rope is attached to the top ring. Floats and a bait box or bait bag complete the equipment. Crab rings lie flat on the bay bottom when dropped and form a basket that holds the crabs when the net is pulled to the surface. The total weight of the rings should be at least eight to ten pounds or the crab nets have a tendency to drift in the heavy Pacific currents and may be lost. The rings are made of sturdy tubular plastic over ⅝-inch steel rod or cable.

Shakin' crabs: a special technique used by professionals and skilled crab crackers to remove intact the delicious meat from the legs of Dungeness crabs. Crabmeat in this attractive form is especially valuable (just as pecan halves are considered more desirable than broken pecan pieces). So, cleaning crabs in Oregon can be summed up by these three little words: backin', crackin', and shakin'.

Star trap: a fairly small and lightweight metal crab trap now found on the west and east coasts—this is the latest in crabbing gear. It is made of a square piece of rust-proof aluminum wire mesh. Four triangles of the same type of wire mesh are connected, the base of each triangle at each side of the square. The star trap unfolds when it is flat on the ground and underwater, but folds up

½ pound minced crabmeat
5 eggs
1 Tbls. cornstarch
2 Tbls. soy sauce
¼ tsp. salt
Dash of white pepper

Blanch the bean sprouts. Sliver the bamboo shoots and onion. Heat 1½ tablespoons of the oil. Add vegetables and stir-fry 1 minute. Transfer to a deep bowl. Add the crabmeat to the vegetables. Beat the eggs and add along with the cornstarch, soy sauce, salt and pepper. Mix well to blend. Heat the remaining 2 tablespoons of oil. Cook the crabmeat mixture about 2 tablespoons at a time, dropping in like pancake batter to form thin cakes. Brown the cakes lightly on each side, turning carefully with a spatula. Repeat, adding more oil if needed. Continue until all crabmeat mixture is finished. Keep the cakes warm until ready to serve. (Note: chopped celery can be substituted for bean sprouts.)

SERVES 4

Greek-American Crab Cakes

3 Tbls. flour
1 pound fresh crabmeat
3 Tbls. mayonnaise
1 Tbls. fresh lemon juice
Salt and pepper to taste
½ cup minced green onions
Bread crumbs
¼ cup olive oil
¼ cup butter
Lemon wedges for garnish

Sprinkle the flour over the crabmeat, then gently mix in mayonnaise, lemon juice, salt, pepper, green onions; stir until stiff enough to form into cakes about ¾-inch-thick. Roll the cakes in bread crumbs and refrigerate several hours. Sauté in olive oil and butter. Serve with lemon wedges.

SERVES 4

Bob Gray's Chesapeake Crab Cakes

2 cups crabmeat
2 cups bread crumbs
2 Tbls. mayonnaise
2 eggs, beaten
2 tsp. lemon juice
Pinch of dry parsley
1 tsp. salt
½ tsp. pepper
½ tsp. dry mustard
½ tsp. paprika
6 drops Tabasco sauce
¼ cup oil
Lemon slices for garnish

Mix all ingredients except last 2 and mold cakes to the desired size. Fry in cooking oil until golden brown. Serve with lemon slices.

SERVES 4

Chesapeake Bay Crab Cakes

2 slices white bread
Milk
1 pound crabmeat
1 Tbls. mayonnaise

quickly when the rope is pulled, catching the unsuspecting crabs while they are feeding on the bait. All the cool sport crabbers use star traps.

Oregon Crab Stories

A wonderful part of American folklore in almost every corner of the country is the legend, especially the tall tale. We expect these from fishermen; after all, that's why we call them "fish stories."

The following stories were collected on a cool and sunny afternoon in June 1994, in front of the office of the Siuslaw Boat Charters by the harbor in Florence, Oregon. A few fishermen were sitting at a picnic table there, hanging out and shooting the breeze. They were more than willing to share their tales with a visiting crab lover from New Orleans.

Here's a story from Tom Wilheight, a fisherman from Florence:

One of the weirdest things to happen out here, not too long ago, happened to a guy on one of the local boats. Well, one day, while he was pullin' crab pots, his wallet fell overboard and was lost. He was real upset because it had his I.D. and a good bit of money in it. The guy was really upset.

Well, about a week later, when he pulled up one of his crab pots, there inside the pot was his very own wallet! And it had all the money and everything in it. It was just the darndest thing!

But, then, you never know what you'll find in them pots. I've pulled up pots that were down one hundred and twenty feet in the ocean and found dead cormorants inside! Now who in the world would believe a cormorant could dive that deep? But they do.

Dannie Owens added that he'd found dead cormorants lots of times in his pots, but usually at much lesser depths. "But," he said, "we always leave them in the pots, 'cause they make real good crab-bait!"

Dannie Owens told the following story, which was embellished by his two cohorts, David Howell and Tom Wilheight:

Now, last summer when things were gettin' a little dull around here, somebody decided to liven things up a bit. One day when we were pullin' up the pots, we found a portable TV set inside one!

1 egg, beaten
1 Tbls. chopped parsley
¼ tsp. salt
1 Tbls. Worcestershire sauce
1 Tbls. baking powder
1 Tbls. Old Bay powder
Lemon slices

Remove the crusts from the bread and break into very small pieces. Moisten bread with milk. Add the remaining ingredients and mix well. Shape into cakes and fry quickly, until golden brown. Serve with lemon slices.

SERVES 3–4

Vicki Long's Surimi Crab Cakes

3 Tbls. mayonnaise
2 eggs, beaten
1 Tbls. fresh lemon juice
½ tsp. dry mustard
½ tsp. Tabasco sauce
3 Tbls. chopped parsley
2 Tbls. minced celery
1 Tbls. minced onion
1 pound surimi (imitation crab meat), chopped
2 cups fresh whole wheat bread crumbs (4 slices of bread processed in blender)
Pam vegetable cooking spray

Combine mayonnaise, eggs, lemon juice, mustard and Tabasco in a large bowl. Stir in the parsley, celery, and onion. Stir in the chopped surimi and bread crumbs. Shape into 8 to 12 patties ½-inch thick. Coat a large, non-stick skillet with Pam. Cook on medium to low heat 5 minutes per side or until brown.

SERVES 4

West Coast Very Spicy Crab Cakes

2 large eggs
½ pound lump crabmeat
1 cup ricotta cheese
1 cup shredded Monterey Jack cheese with jalapeños
3 Tbls. chopped chives
¾ cup seasoned bread crumbs
¼ cup light salad oil
1 7-ounce jar roasted red peppers, drained
⅓ cup mayonnaise

In medium bowl beat eggs. Stir in crab, ricotta and Monterey Jack cheeses, chives, and ¼ cup of the bread crumbs. Form heaping tablespoonfuls of crab mixture into ¼-inch-thick cakes. On a sheet of waxed paper, coat the cakes with the remaining bread crumbs. Preheat the oven to 325°. Line baking sheet with paper towels. In a large skillet, heat oil over medium heat. In hot oil, fry crab cakes, a few at a time, until golden on both sides. As cakes cook, remove from pan, drain on prepared baking sheet, and keep warm in oven. In food processor, process red peppers with mayonnaise until smooth. Serve with the crab cakes.

SERVES 4

Cajun Crab Imperial

½ green pepper, minced
2 Tbls. chopped pimento
1 tsp. dry mustard
¼ tsp. white pepper
1 raw egg
⅓ cup mayonnaise
¾ tsp. salt
1 pound crabmeat

Now, we find lots of strange things inside the pots, sneakers, socks, and big whale bones, but a TV set? For a while there, before the pot came to the top, we sure thought we'd caught a lot of crabs.

We knew it was a prank. So, of course, we put the TV in somebody else's pot, and so on, and so forth. That TV set went from pot to pot all summer—it really made the rounds.

Another time we passed close to another boat and all the guys egged us [threw raw eggs at them]. But, we got even with them. A few days later, we pulled up some of their pots when they weren't around and put dead starfish in 'em [dead starfish really stink] and then we wired their pots closed! They must have had a great time unwiring their traps to get the dead starfish out, with all that stink!

These fishermen explained that the work of ocean crabbing is very taxing. In the dead of winter, they leave port in the dark and return in the dark, spending long, cold days doing wet, demanding work on an unstable platform, above an unforgiving ocean. The reward can range from a bumper catch to so few crabs that even fuel costs aren't met.

They also pointed out that ocean crabbing is boring and monotonous work. They said pranks like the "Travelling TV Set" and the "Dead Starfish Wired-into-the-Other-Guys'-Pot" are just good-natured horseplay meant to liven up the dull times spent out on the high seas.

Native American Folklore

The heroes in Native North American mythology are usually tricksters, including characters known as Coyote, Rabbit, and Raven. On the one hand, they provide mankind with many needed items like drinking water, fire, and food; on the other hand, they often act foolishly and unpredictably. Sometimes quite humorous, they are also important supernatural beings.

Dungeness and king crabs were heavily used in the diet of Native Americans of the northwest coast of North America. The following is a Tillamook Indian legend translated as "The Crabs." It was collected by May Edel near the small town of Garibaldi, Oregon, in the early 1930s. It is reprinted

2 Tbls. melted butter
Mayonnaise
Paprika

Combine first 9 ingredients, taking care not to break up the lumps of crabmeat; toss lightly. Divide mixture into 4 portions and place in separate casseroles (large sea shells or crab shells make attractive serving dishes). Coat each serving with a light topping of mayonnaise and sprinkle with paprika. Bake at 300° for about 20 minutes.

SERVES 4

Chesapeake Bay Crab Imperial

3 Tbls. butter, divided
1 Tbls. minced onion
1 Tbls. flour
½ cup milk
1½ tsp. Worcestershire sauce
2 slices white bread, crusts removed, cubed
½ cup mayonnaise
1 Tbls. fresh lemon juice
½ tsp. salt
Pepper to taste
1 pound lump crabmeat
Paprika

In medium pan, melt 1 tablespoon of the butter and sauté onion until soft. Mix in flour. Slowly add milk, stirring constantly to keep mixture smooth and free from lumps. Cook, stirring, over medium heat until mixture comes to a boil and thickens. Remove from heat and stir in Worcestershire and bread crumbs. Cool. Fold in mayonnaise, lemon juice, salt, and pepper. In another pan, heat remaining 2 tablespoons butter until lightly browned. Add crabmeat and toss lightly. Combine with sauce mixture, being very careful not to break up the crabmeat. Put mixture into individual shells or ramekins (or greased 1-quart casserole). Sprinkle paprika over top. Bake at 450° until hot and bubbly and lightly browned on top, 10 to 15 minutes.

SERVES 4

Southern Crabmeat au Gratin

½ cup chopped green onions
2 Tbls. chopped celery
½ cup chopped mushrooms
3 Tbls. butter
1 cup thick white sauce
1 pound lump crabmeat
Salt and pepper to taste
1 cup American cheese, grated
Black olive halves and lemon wedges for garnish

Sauté chopped green onions, celery, and mushrooms in butter. Add white sauce, crabmeat, salt and pepper. Place in buttered baking dish, top with grated cheese and bake at 350° until cheese turns brown, about 20 to 25 minutes. Garnish with black olive halves and wedges of lemon.

SERVES 4

White Sauce
¼ cup butter
¼ cup flour
1 cup scalded milk
Salt and pepper to taste

Melt butter in heavy saucepan; blend in flour on low heat, stirring constantly until smooth. Remove from heat; stir in the

through the courtesy of M. Terry Thompson. I have taken the liberty to reword, in just a few places, the original translation.

The story emphasizes the importance of crabs as a food source. A rich supply for the native people was insured by a brave act of Rabbit, an important trickster character. Small and defenseless as he was, Rabbit went against the strong and powerful Chief of the Crab People to provide food for his starving people, and for all humankind.

The Crabs
Rabbit had no mother, only a grandmother. She raised him. Rabbit was small and hungry. The people were all starving. There was no food. His grandmother went for crabs but there were only little ones. The rest of the people hardly got any catch.

Finally, his grandmother returned. The old lady baked the little crabs she had gathered, and Rabbit tore off their backs to eat them. He said, "Oh, I don't want these crabs. They are bad. They have disgusting little hips."

So his grandmother said to him, "You talk pretty bad. You better go on a power fast. Then you'll get a strong power and you'll kill the person who puts up all the fences around the big crabs so we can't get to them. Then we will get good crabs."

Soon Rabbit went fasting. Then after a while Rabbit came back to his grandmother. He said, "Grandmother, soon I'm going to kill this bad person. Finally I shall break up his fence and there will be many crabs crawling about."

The old woman said, "Oh, you're just lying."

He said, "Really, now I shall go."

So he went and killed this man [the Chief of the Crab People]. Rabbit killed him. Then he called the Crab People. He said, "Now, come ashore. Your master is no more. I myself killed your Chief."

Then all the Crab People came ashore.

Rabbit went back to his grandmother. He said, "Grandmother, you won't have to go to the ocean to get crabs anymore. There will be crabs all over. There will be many crabs right here."

Then that woman really saw the crabs. There were lots of them and she believed it all.

Rabbit said, "Never in the time to come will one man take all the crabs. Everyone will have these crabs."

heated milk a little at a time. Season to taste and cook over low heat until thick and bubbly.

Cajun Crabmeat au Gratin

1¼ cup minced onion
1 stalk celery, minced
¼ pound margarine
½ cup all-purpose flour
1 13-ounce can evaporated milk
2 egg yolks
2 tsp. salt
½ tsp. cayenne
¼ tsp. black pepper
1 pound crabmeat
½ pound Cheddar cheese, grated

Sauté onion and celery in margarine until transparent and wilted. Add flour and blend well, still stirring. Pour in milk gradually, stirring constantly. Add egg yolks, salt, cayenne and black pepper; cook about 5 minutes. Put crabmeat in a mixing bowl and pour the cooked sauce over it. Blend well; put mixture in a lightly greased casserole and sprinkle with grated Cheddar cheese. Bake at 375° for 10 or 15 minutes or until cheese turns light brown.
SERVES 4

Cajun Easy Crabmeat au Gratin

1 cup flaked crabmeat
1 Tbls. butter, plus more for topping
2 green onions, chopped
½ cup hollandaise sauce
Grated Parmesan cheese

Heat crabmeat in 1 tablespoon of the butter with green onions and hollandaise sauce; place in individual baking dishes. Top with freshly grated Parmesan cheese and butter; bake at 375° until cheese is brown.

SERVES 2

Hollandaise Sauce

¼ pound butter
4 egg yolks, beaten
2 tsp. lemon juice
White pepper and salt

Heat butter in top of double boiler over simmering, NOT boiling, water. Stir constantly while adding egg yolks; add lemon juice and seasonings. Cook until thickened.

Southern Crab au Gratin with Grits

Instant grits may be substituted for the following recipe since they are quite good and easy to make. Cook enough to make about 4 cups of cooked grits.

Grits

1 cup hominy grits
4 cups boiling water
1 tsp. salt
1 Tbls. butter

Pour grits into boiling salted water and stir until it returns to a boil. Lower heat and simmer slowly for an hour, stirring frequently. When ready, add the butter and beat well for a few minutes. Keep warm.

Greek Folklore

There is a delightful Greek folksong entitled "The Baby Crabs" ("*Ta Kavourakia*"), reminiscent of "The Walrus and the Carpenter," a poem by Lewis Carroll. In it, the demise of the baby crabs is blamed on their naughty mother, Mrs. Crab, not the true culprit—a hungry predator named Sparos (a Mediterranean fish that eats crabs).

The Baby Crabs
On the beach atop the small
    pebbles
are sitting two baby crabs,
    abandoned,
crying sorrowfully of their
    misery.

And meanwhile their mother,
    Mrs. Crab,
is out having an affair with
    Sparos in Rafina,
And the little crabs are crying
    sorrowfully
on the pebbles on the beach.

As the sun rises and the sky
    turns purple,
Mr. Crab returns from a hard
    night of work.
Unable to find his wife and
    babies,
he pulls out all of his hair.

Meanwhile Mrs. Crab and
Sparos are entwined,
watching the sunrise in Rafina.
And still the baby crabs are
crying sorrowfully
atop the pebbles on the beach.

Years ago on the island of
Crete, I collected a little joke
about the duplicity of politi-
cians. It also makes fun of shep-
herds, who are stereotyped as
rubes in Greek humor, and it
features a crab:

A forty-something-year-old
shepherd from the mountain village of Anogia went down to the
seashore for the first time. Well, on
the beach he found a crab. He had
never seen a crab before, and it
frightened him. But he took courage, grabbed his backpack from his
shoulder, and threw it on top of the
crab and caught it.

"I'll take this wild beast to the
mayor of our village," he thought
to himself. "He'll know what it is!"

So he went back up the moun-
tains to his village, telling people all
along the way that he had caught
a terrible wild beast. He went
straight away to the mayor's house.
When he got inside, he opened the
backpack and dropped the crab
onto the floor.

The mayor also had never seen

Crab au Gratin

2 Tbls. butter
2 cups crabmeat
Salt and pepper to taste
½ cup evaporated milk
2 well-beaten egg yolks
½ cup grated Cheddar cheese

Melt the butter; add the crabmeat, salt, and pepper, and
cook for 5 minutes without browning. Mix the evaporated milk
with the egg yolks. Add to hot crabmeat and cook for 4 minutes over low heat, stirring constantly. Butter 4 to 6 ramekins
and spread the grits over the bottoms. (The grits also may be
placed inside a large, buttered, square baking dish.) Cover with
the crab mixture. Sprinkle the cheese on top and bake in 350°
oven until cheese turns golden brown. Serve immediately.
SERVES 4–6

East Coast Crab and Cheese Bake

2 eggs
1 tsp. flour
½ pound crabmeat
1 cup heavy cream
1 cup grated Swiss cheese
1 cup grated Cheddar cheese
1 tsp. Accent
Salt and pepper to taste

Preheat oven to 325°. Beat eggs. Add remaining ingredients,
stirring well. Pour into 9-inch pie plate. Bake 1 hour.
SERVES 6

Caribbean Crab Pudding

1 Tbls. minced green onions
3 Tbls. butter
1/4 cup flour
2 cups light cream
2 egg yolks
1 pound crabmeat
1/8 tsp. ground nutmeg
Pinch cayenne pepper
1/2 pound Münster cheese, thinly sliced
3 egg whites
1/2 tsp. salt
1/4 tsp. white pepper
2 Tbls. grated Parmesan cheese

Preheat oven to 350°. Sauté the green onions in the melted butter in a 3-quart saucepan. Stir in the flour and cook, stirring constantly, for a minute or two. Slowly add the cream, stirring with a whisk. Cook over a high heat, still stirring, until sauce comes to a boil. Reduce heat and simmer for 2 minutes. Beat the egg yolks one at a time into the sauce and return to a boil. Stir while boiling for 30 seconds. Remove from heat, stir in the crabmeat, nutmeg and a pinch of cayenne pepper.

Spoon half of the crab mixture into a greased 2-quart casserole. Spread with half of the Münster cheese slices. Spoon in the rest of the crab mixture and cover with remaining cheese.

In a large bowl, beat the egg whites, salt, and white pepper with an electric mixer until they make firm peaks. Gently spread this over the sliced cheese and sprinkle the top with the grated Parmesan cheese.

Bake for 25 minutes or until the meringue is golden. Serve immediately.

SERVES 4

a crab before, but, as is typical of pompous persons, he didn't admit his ignorance.

The crab began to scurry forward, so quickly the shepherd grabbed a piece of firewood to block its path. Then, the crab began walking backwards, and the shepherd put another piece of wood behind it to block its escape. The crab then started moving forward again.

Just then, someone came into the mayor's house and said: "I want to see the wild beast that the whole village is talking about. What's it called?"

The mayor, with the air of an expert marine zoologist, announced: "It's called a round trip!"

A final bit of Greek lore is the following rhyme, known to children on the island of Chios:

The Crab's Invitation
Down on the beach in the sand,
the crabs are having a wedding.
They invited me to go
to dance and to eat.

One wonders what will be served for lunch.

Southern Crab Soufflé

3 Tbls. butter
2 Tbls. grated onion
3 Tbls. flour
2/3 cup milk, scalded
3 egg yolks, lightly beaten
1 Tbl. parsley, minced
2 tsp. lemon juice
3/4 tsp. plus 1/8 tsp. salt
1/2 tsp. paprika
Pepper to taste
1 1/4 cups lump crabmeat
4 egg whites
Hollandaise sauce (optional)*

Butter a 5-cup soufflé dish. Tie a 10-inch-long doubled and buttered piece of waxed paper around the top to form a 2-inch collar. Set dish aside. Preheat oven to 350°. In a saucepan, sauté onion in butter for one minute. Add flour gradually, stirring constantly. Remove pan from heat and gradually stir in scalded milk (milk that has been brought to a full boil); cook two minutes. Transfer sauce to a bowl and blend in egg yolks, parsley, lemon juice, 3/4 tsp. salt, paprika, and pepper. Gently stir in crabmeat. In another bowl, combine egg whites and 1/8 tsp. salt; beat until stiff. Fold 1/4 egg whites into crab mixture; fold this mixture into remaining egg whites. Spoon mixture into prepared dish and bake 35 to 40 minutes. Serve with hollandaise sauce if desired.

*See Cajun Easy Crabmeat au Gratin (page 114) for hollandaise sauce recipe.

SERVES 4–6

Louisiana Almond and Crab Casserole

1 cup crabmeat
1 cup cooked, peeled shrimp
2 cans mushroom soup, undiluted
1 cup finely sliced celery
¼ cup minced onion
1 3-ounce can crisp fried noodles
2 ounces shaved almonds

Combine crabmeat, chopped shrimp, mushroom soup, celery, onion, and crisp noodles. Turn into a greased casserole and sprinkle almonds over the top. Bake at 375° for 25 minutes.

SERVES 4–6

Cajun Crab Casserole with Potato Chips

¼ cup chopped green onions
¼ pound butter
White sauce*
½ cup dry white wine
Salt and cayenne to taste
½ pound grated Swiss cheese
1 pound crabmeat
2 cups crushed potato chips

Sauté the green onions in the butter until wilted. Make a white sauce; add the wine, seasonings, and cheese; stir until the cheese has melted. Fold in the crabmeat. Top with crushed potato chips and bake uncovered at 350° for 20 minutes.

*See Southern Crabmeat au Gratin (page 112) for white sauce recipe.

SERVES 4–6

Cajun Crab Casserole with Cheddar Cheese

1 onion, chopped
1 celery stalk, chopped
¼ pound margarine
½ cup sifted flour
1 13-ounce can evaporated milk
2 egg yolks
1 pound crabmeat
3 green onions, minced
½ pound Cheddar cheese, grated
Salt and pepper to taste

Sauté the white onion and celery in the margarine until wilted; stir in the flour well, but do not brown. Pour in the milk, stirring constantly. Add the egg yolks, salt, and pepper and cook 5 minutes until thick. Add the crabmeat and the green onions and mix well. Pour into a greased baking dish and cover with grated Cheddar cheese. Bake uncovered at 375° until the cheese has browned.

SERVES 4–6

Crab-Rice Casserole

2 cups cooked rice
1 can water chestnuts
½ cup cooked, peeled shrimp
1 cup dry white wine
½ cup crabmeat
1 cup mayonnaise
1 cup finely sliced celery
½ cup sliced almonds
½ cup chopped onions
1 cup grated Cheddar cheese
Salt and pepper to taste

Mix all ingredients together in a large casserole dish. Bake at 350° for 30 minutes and serve.

SERVES 6

Cajun Crab Casserole with Shrimp

4 ounces cream cheese
4 Tbls. butter, divided
1 pound peeled raw shrimp
1 cup chopped onions
1/2 cup chopped celery
1/2 cup chopped green pepper
1 can golden mushroom soup
1/4 cup pimentos
1/2 tsp. cayenne pepper
1 Tbls. garlic salt
1 tsp. Tabasco sauce
1 pint crabmeat
2 cups cooked rice
1/2 cup buttered bread crumbs
1/4 cup grated Cheddar cheese

Melt cream cheese and 2 tablespoons of the butter in double boiler. Melt remaining 2 tablespoons of butter in skillet and sauté shrimp over a low fire until they turn light pink, about 3 to 5 minutes. Add onion, celery, and green pepper and continue to sauté until vegetables are slightly wilted. Add melted cream cheese, butter and mushroom soup; mix well. Add pimentos, seasonings, crabmeat and rice; mix well and place in a 2-quart casserole. Top with bread crumbs and Cheddar cheese. Bake uncovered at 350° for 20 to 30 minutes.

SERVES 6–8

Southern Crab Casserole with Asparagus

1 15-ounce can asparagus
½ pound crabmeat
1 can cream of mushroom soup
3 cups cooked rice
½ cup mayonnaise
1 tsp. fresh lemon juice
Salt and pepper to taste
¼ cup grated Parmesan cheese
Buttered bread crumbs

Arrange the asparagus, cut into 1-inch lengths, in a large casserole. Flake the crabmeat and place over the asparagus. Combine soup, rice, mayonnaise, lemon juice, salt, and pepper. Pour over the crab. Top with cheese and crumbs. Bake at 350° for about 25 minutes.

SERVES 6–8

Creole Crab Casserole with Artichoke Hearts

1 small onion, chopped
1 garlic clove, minced
2 Tbls. butter or margarine
2 Tbls. flour
1 cup milk
1 egg yolk, beaten
1 tsp. horseradish
3 Tbls. minced parsley
Salt to taste
Cayenne pepper to taste
1 pound crabmeat
2 Tbls. fresh lemon juice
1 tsp. Worcestershire sauce

1 can artichoke hearts, broken up
½ cup bread crumbs

Sauté the onion and garlic in the melted butter until wilted. Blend in the flour; add the milk gradually, stirring until thickened. Remove from heat; add egg yolk, horseradish, chopped parsley, salt, and cayenne pepper, and blend well. Add the crabmeat, lemon juice, Worcestershire sauce, and artichoke hearts. Put in a shallow casserole and top with bread crumbs and the minced parsley. Bake at 350° about 20 minutes.

SERVES 6

Southern Crab Casserole with Mushrooms and Artichokes

1 large can artichoke hearts
1 can (4 ounces) sliced mushrooms
1 pound crabmeat
2 Tbls. butter or margarine
2½ Tbls. flour
½ tsp. salt
⅛ tsp. cayenne pepper
1 cup half-and-half cream
2 Tbls. dry sherry
2 Tbls. seasoned bread crumbs
1 Tbls. grated Parmesan cheese
Paprika
Cooked rice

Drain the liquid from the artichokes and mushrooms. Cut artichokes in half and place in a well-greased, shallow 1½-quart casserole. Cover with mushrooms and crabmeat. Melt margarine in a saucepan. Blend in flour, salt, cayenne. Add cream gradually and cook until thick, stirring constantly. Stir in sherry. Pour sauce over crabmeat. Combine crumbs and cheese, and sprinkle over sauce. Sprinkle with paprika. Bake in a hot 450° oven for 12 to 15 minutes or until bubbly. Serve over cooked white rice.

SERVES 6

Southern Crab Casserole with Crackers

2 Tbls. butter, plus more for topping
1 pack Waverly Crackers, crushed
1 pound crabmeat
1 small onion, chopped
1 small green pepper, chopped
Lemon juice
Salt to taste
1 pint half-and-half cream

Grease the casserole dish with the butter. Mix the crumbled crackers with the crabmeat. Finely chop the onion and green pepper and sprinkle on top of mixture. Sprinkle with a little lemon juice and salt; dot with butter. Pour the cream over the mixture and bake at 325° for 25 minutes.

SERVES 6

Cajun Basic Crab Casserole

1 large onion, minced
3 stalks celery, chopped
1 stick butter
1 pound crabmeat
2 eggs
1 slice bread
1 bunch green onions, chopped
2 Tbls. chopped parsley
1 Tbls. Worcestershire sauce

Salt and cayenne pepper
Buttered bread crumbs

Sauté onion and celery in butter until wilted. Add crabmeat and heat. Beat eggs. Add bread that has been first soaked in water, squeezed, then broken into small pieces. Beat together; then add to the crabmeat. Add all other ingredients, except bread crumbs, and heat thoroughly. Place in a buttered casserole or individual shells. Top with buttered bread crumbs. Bake at 350° about 20 minutes.

SERVES 4–6

East Coast Open-Face Crabmeat Sandwiches

½ pound crabmeat
¼ cup mayonnaise
3 split English muffins
2 Tbls. margarine
1 3-ounce package cream cheese, softened
1 egg yolk
2 tsp. minced onion
¼ tsp. prepared mustard
Salt and pepper to taste

Preheat broiler. Mix crabmeat with mayonnaise; set aside. Spread muffins with margarine; toast until brown. Mix cream cheese, egg yolk, onion, mustard, salt, and pepper; beat well. Spread muffins with crabmeat and cover with cheese mixture. Place on baking sheet. Broil 5 inches from heating element for 2 to 3 minutes or until lightly browned and puffed.

MAKES 6 portions

West Coast Crabmeat Sandwiches

½ pound crabmeat
2 tsp. minced onion
2 tsp. minced green pepper
¼ tsp. prepared mustard
Salt and pepper to taste
¼ cup mayonnaise
6 slices sourdough bread
2 Tbls. margarine
3 ounces Monterey Jack cheese or Tillamook Cheddar, grated

Preheat broiler. Mix crabmeat with onion, green pepper, mustard, salt, pepper, and mayonnaise; set aside. Spread bread with margarine; toast until brown. Spread bread with crabmeat mixture. Cover with grated cheese. Place on baking sheet. Broil 5 inches from heating element for 2 to 3 minutes or until lightly browned and puffed.

MAKES 6 portions

Alaskan Crab Burgers

1 pound Alaskan king crab
1 egg
2 slices white bread
1 tsp. lemon juice
¼ cup onion
½ tsp. salt
¼ tsp. pepper
Few sprigs fresh dill or parsley

Put all ingredients into a food processor and mix. Make into patties and fry in buttered skillet, enough to warm crabmeat. Serve on toasted buns with lettuce and mayonnaise or tartar sauce. (Recipe courtesy of the Alaska Department of Fish and Game.)

SERVES 4

Southern Crab Quiche

1 9-inch pie crust
½ cup mayonnaise
½ pound Swiss cheese, cut in chunks
2 Tbls. flour
½ pound crabmeat
½ cup chopped green onion
2 eggs, beaten
½ cup milk
¼ tsp. salt
¼ cup parsley
Lemon juice to taste
Paprika for garnish

Cook the pie crust until slightly browned. Combine all ingredients except lemon juice, parsley, and paprika. Mix well. Place in pie shell and bake at 350° for 30 to 40 minutes. Remove from oven and sprinkle with lemon juice, parsley and paprika.

SERVES 6–8

Florida Microwave Crab Quiche

1 unbaked deep-dish pie shell
1 tsp. Worcestershire sauce
1 cup grated Swiss cheese
1 pound crabmeat
¾ cup sliced ripe olives
3 eggs, slightly beaten
1 cup half-and-half

¼ cup chopped green onions
½ tsp. salt
5–6 drops Tabasco sauce
Paprika

Place the pie shell in a deep-dish ceramic or glass pie plate, pressing the dough firmly against the sides to prevent shrinkage during cooking. Sprinkle the Worcestershire sauce over the crust and spread evenly with a pastry brush. Prick the dough with a fork in several places. Microwave on HIGH for 3 minutes or until done. Let cool. Sprinkle the cheese over the bottom of the pie shell. Add the crab and ripe olives. Mix eggs, half-and-half, onions, salt, and Tabasco together and pour over crab and olives. Sprinkle with paprika. Microwave on HIGH 15 to 18 minutes, rotating the dish a quarter turn every 3 minutes. To test the quiche for doneness, insert a knife in the center. It is done when the knife comes out clean. Let stand 2 minutes. May be served hot or at room temperature. (Courtesy of the Florida Department of Agriculture and Consumer Services, Bureau of Seafood and Aquaculture.)

SERVES 8

Southern Crabmeat Pie

1 9-inch pie shell
1 cup grated Swiss cheese
½ pound crabmeat
2 green onions, chopped
2 eggs
¾ cup of milk or cream
½ tsp. salt
¼ tsp. dry mustard
½ tsp. grated lemon peel
Sliced almonds or Chinese noodles

Bake pie shell for 10 minutes and cool. Sprinkle grated cheese over pie shell; top with flaked crabmeat and green onions. Beat eggs; add milk with seasonings and mix together; pour mixture over other ingredients in pie shell. Top with almonds or crumbled Chinese noodles. Bake at 325° about 50 minutes.

SERVES 6–8

West Coast Deep-Dish Crab Pie

½ cup carrots, chopped
2 Tbls. butter
¼ cup chopped green onions
1 tsp. dill weed
1 tsp. basil
1 pound crabmeat
1 raw pie shell in 10-inch quiche pan
1 13-ounce can evaporated milk
5 eggs
3 Tbls. dry sherry
1 tsp. prepared mustard
½ tsp. salt

Sauté the carrots in the butter until tender. Add onions, dill weed, and basil; cook about 1 minute. Remove from heat and stir in the crabmeat. Spoon into pie shell. Beat remaining ingredients and pour over crab mixture. Bake on bottom rack of preheated 325° oven for 50 to 55 minutes. Let cool for 15 minutes.

SERVES 8

Oregon Crabmeat and Herb Tart

1 tube refrigerated dough for pizza or 1 package pizza crust mix
1 medium tomato, chopped
½ medium onion, chopped
¼ cup grated Parmesan cheese
½ pound king crab chunks
4 eggs
3 Tbls. water
2 tsp. prepared mustard
½ tsp. seasoned salt

Spread dough on bottom and halfway up sides of greased 13- x 9-inch baking dish. Top with tomato, onion, Parmesan cheese and crabmeat. Mix eggs, water, mustard, and seasoned salt in small bowl. Pour over crabmeat and vegetables. Bake in 375° oven for 25 minutes or until eggs are set and puffed in the center. Let stand 5 minutes before cutting.

SERVES 8

East Coast Crab and Avocado Quiche

1 9-inch pie shell
¼ pound crabmeat
2 tsp. fresh lemon juice
4 eggs
1½ cups milk
½ cup dry white wine
Pinch dill weed
¼ tsp. salt
Pinch black pepper
1 ripe avocado

Preheat oven to 400°. Precook pie shell for 10 minutes before adding filling; then lower the oven to 350°. Toss the crabmeat in a small bowl with lemon juice, and spread mixture evenly on the bottom of the precooked crust. Beat the eggs and milk together and add the wine. Beat until frothy. Pour over the crab mixture and sprinkle lightly with dill, salt, and freshly ground black pepper. Bake for 30 to 40 minutes or until knife inserted in center comes out clean. Slice avocado and arrange on top of the quiche. Serve immediately.

SERVES 6–8

Alaskan Quick King Crab Fondue

1 ½ pounds Alaska king crab
1 clove garlic, peeled
2 10¾-ounce cans condensed Cheddar cheese soup
½ cup sour cream
¼ cup dry white wine

Slice king crab legs into pieces large enough for dunking, and set aside. Rub chafing dish or electric skillet with peeled and cut clove of garlic. Pour in soup and sour cream. Heat, stirring until smooth; gradually add wine. Heat, but do not boil. Keep fondue hot while serving. Serve with pieces of Alaska king crab for dunking. Second-day treat: add small pieces of crab to any remaining fondue and serve over toast points. (Recipe courtesy Alaska Department of Fish and Game.)

SERVES 6–8

Chinese Stir-Fried Crabmeat with Eggs

4 eggs
1 cup chicken broth
2 Tbls. light soy sauce
1 pound crabmeat

1½ Tbls. dry sherry
1 tsp. sugar
Salt to taste
1½ Tbls. cornstarch
¼ cup water
½ cup peanut or corn oil
2 Tbls. minced fresh ginger
3 Tbls. chopped green onion
1½ Tbls. red wine vinegar

Beat the eggs in a mixing bowl and add chicken broth, soy sauce, and crabmeat. Stir and set aside. In a separate container, blend together the sherry, sugar and salt; set aside. Blend together the cornstarch and water; set aside. Heat 3 tablespoons of the oil in a small saucepan and add the ginger. Cook briefly, then set aside. Heat the remaining oil in a wok or skillet and add the egg and crab mixture. Stir very gently and slowly to cook. After about 1½ minutes, when it starts to set, add the ginger and wine mixture and stir. After cooking about 2½ to 3 minutes, add the green onions and the cornstarch mixture. Stir in the vinegar. The total cooking time for the egg and crab mixture should be about 4 to 5 minutes, no longer. When cooked, spoon the mixture onto a warm serving dish.

SERVES 4

Chinese Basic Stir-Fried Crabmeat

3–4 green onion stalks
2 slices fresh ginger root, peeled
2 Tbls. soy sauce
2 Tbls. dry sherry
½ tsp. salt
2 Tbls. peanut or corn oil
1 pound crabmeat
1 Tbls. cornstarch
¼ cup water

Cut green onions into ½-inch sections. Mince ginger root slices. Combine soy sauce, sherry, and salt. Heat oil. Add crabmeat and minced ginger root; stir-fry about 1 minute over medium heat. Add green onion sections; stir-fry a few times more. Stir in soy-sherry mixture and heat quickly. Simmer, covered, 2 to 3 minutes. Meanwhile, blend cornstarch and cold water to a paste; then stir in to thicken. Serve at once.

SERVES 4

Chinese Stir-Fried Crabmeat with Shrimp

1 pound crabmeat
2 Tbls. minced fresh ginger
2 Tbls. chopped green onions
1 cup chopped raw shrimp
1 Tbls. plus 2 tsp. cornstarch
3 Tbls. water
2 cups peanut or corn oil
4 cloves garlic, crushed
2 Tbls. dry sherry
½ cup chicken broth
½ tsp. sugar
1 Tbls. light soy sauce
1 Tbls. dark soy sauce
¼ cup green onions cut into 1-inch lengths
¼ tsp. fine white pepper

Mix the crabmeat with half the ginger and all the chopped green onions. Set aside. Blend the shrimp with the 2 teaspoons cornstarch and mix well. Set aside. Blend the remaining 1 tablespoon of cornstarch with the water and set aside. Heat the oil in a wok or skillet. When warm, add the shrimp and cook, stirring, for 30 seconds. Drain in a sieve-lined bowl to catch the drippings, leaving 3 tablespoons of oil in the pan. Add the garlic to the oil and brown; remove and discard garlic. Add the crab mixture and cook, stirring, about 30 seconds; add the sherry. Cook 30 seconds and add the chicken broth. Immediately add the sugar and soy sauces. Cook 1 minute and add the cornstarch-water mixture. Cook just until thickened; add the shrimp and cook about 30 seconds to finish cooking the shrimp. Turn out onto a serving plate and serve sprinkled with the remaining ginger, green onions, and white pepper.

SERVES 4–6

Chinese Simmered Crabs with Pork

2 crabs, uncooked
1 cup chicken stock
2 Tbls. soy sauce
1 tsp. sugar
1/2 tsp. salt, divided
1/2 tsp. white pepper
4 Tbls. peanut or corn oil
1 clove garlic, crushed
1/4 pound lean ground pork
1 Tbls. cornstarch
1/4 cup water
1 egg, lightly beaten
2 green onions, minced

Remove the backs and clean the crabs as in the Buddy Touard method (see p. 14). With a cleaver, chop each crab, shell and all, into 6 or 8 pieces. Heat the chicken stock and stir in soy sauce, sugar, 1/4 teaspoon of the salt, and pepper. Set aside but keep warm. Heat the oil; add the remaining salt and then garlic, and stir-fry a few times. Add the pork and stir-fry until it loses its pinkness (1 to 2 minutes). Stir in the stock mixture; add the crab sections and heat quickly. Cook, covered, 8 to 10 minutes over medium heat. Meanwhile, blend cornstarch and cold water to a paste. Add and stir into the crab mixture to thicken. Turn off the heat. Gently stir in the beaten egg until it sets. Garnish with chopped scallions and serve.

SERVES 2

Chinese Stir-Fried Crabmeat with Pork

2 Tbls. soy sauce
2 Tbls. dry sherry
2 Tbls. water
½ tsp. salt
½ tsp. sugar
2–3 Tbls. peanut or corn oil
¼ pound ground lean pork
1 pound crabmeat
2 Tbls. minced fresh ginger root
2 eggs, lightly beaten
2 green onions, minced

Combine soy sauce, sherry, water, salt, and sugar. Set aside. Heat oil. Add pork and stir-fry until it loses its pinkness (1 to 2 minutes). Add crabmeat and ginger; stir-fry a few times. Then gently stir in eggs. Add soy-sherry mixture and cook, stirring, over low heat 3 to 4 minutes. Garnish with chopped green onions and serve immediately.

SERVES 3–4

References

Allen, Richard H. *Star Names: Their Lore and Meaning.* New York: Dover Publications, Inc., 1963.

Beebe, William. *Bahias de America: cronica de un viaje cientihifico.* Buenos Aires: Atlandida, S.A., 1944.

Banister, Keith and A. Campbell. *The Encyclopedia of Aquatic Life.* Oxford, England: Equinox, Ltd., 1985.

Blau, S. Forrest. "King Crabs: A Golden Resource." *Alaska Fish and Game* 22, No. 1 (1990): 2–6.

Demory, Darrell. "Crabbing: Commercial and Sport." *Oregon Wildlife* (October 1979): 3–7.

Didier, Al J., ed. *A Review of the California, Oregon, and Washington Dungeness Crab Fishery.* Gladstone, Oregon: Pacific States Marine Fisheries Commission, 1993.

Donner, Christopher. "Tales From a Peruvian Crypt" *Natural History* 10, no. 5 (1994): 26–36.

Elwin, Verrier. *The Agaria.* Calcutta, India: Oxford University Press, 1942.

———. *The Myths of Middle India.* Oxford, England: Oxford University Press, 1949.

———. *Tribal Myths of Orissa.* New York: Arno Press, 1980.

Fagan, Brian M. *Kingdoms of Gold, Kingdoms of Jade: The Americas Before Columbus.* New York: Thames and Hudson, Ltd., 1991.

Grzimeh, Bernard. *Animal Life Encyclopedia.* New York: Van Nostrand, 1984.

Jaworski, Eugene. *Biogeography of the Blue Crab Fishery, Barataria Estuary, Louisiana.* Ann Arbor, Michigan: University Microfilms, 1985.

Lothrop, Samuel K. *Coclé: An Archeological Study of Central Panama.* Cambridge: Memoirs of the Peabody Museum of Archeology and Ethnology, VIII, 1942.

MacNeice, Louis. *Astrology.* London: Aldus Books Ltd., 1964.

MacQueen, Steve. "Crabs, Mullet and History Make for Seaside Fun." *Tallahassee Democrat* (May 6, 1994), 18D.

Meacham, Chuck. "Commercial Fisheries: Alaska Ranks First." *Alaska's Wildlife* 24, no.2 (1992): 2–6.

Morris, Robert M., et al. *Intertidal Invertebrates of California.* Stanford: Stanford University Press, 1980.

Snow, C. Dale. "Interesting Crabs of Oregon." *Oregon Wildlife* (April 1978): 3–6.

Thompson, C. J. S. *The Mystery and Romance of Astrology.* Detroit: Singing Tree Press, 1969.

Warner, William W. *Beautiful Swimmers.* New York: Penguin Books, 1976.

Recipe Index